"We often forget that the Christian walk is not merely about getting us into heaven, but it is also about getting heaven into us. This is why our Lord gave us the Beatitudes, the Sermon on the Mount, and the parable of the Good Samaritan. Thus, it is no surprise that the apostle James offers this injunction to the Early Church: 'Pure religion and undefiled before God and the Father is this, To visit the fatherless and widows in their affliction, and to keep himself unspotted from the world' (James 1:27, KJV). In this wonderful monograph, *Adopted for Life*, Russell Moore offers to the Christian world a compelling account of these and other lessons of Scripture so that our communities of faith may put them into practice and become more like that 'shining city on a hill' of which our Lord spoke."

> —FRANCIS J. BECKWITH, Professor of Philosophy and Church-State Studies, Baylor University; author of *Defending Life: A Moral and Legal Case Against Abortion Choice*

"Russell Moore's life has validated every word he has written. But most especially, his father's heart has been vulnerable and broken. In this book he speaks from his heart, mind, and life to ours about the possibility of incarnating adoption as a fleshed out reality in the world of our own families."

> —MICHAEL CARD, musician and Bible teacher

"Russell Moore reminds us in his powerful book *Adopted for Life* that the true Christian family reaches far beyond the biological. The poignant tale of the adoption of two Russian orphans by him and his wife Maria grows into a metaphor of Christian salvation. This book offers both practical advice and courage to every couple considering adoption. For all readers, it shows how the act of adoption actually reveals core truths about the gospel of Christ."

> —ALLAN CARLSON, President, the Howard Center for Family, Religion & Society

"Russell Moore, who is one of the bright young leaders in the Christian world, combines his own experience of adopting sons with a powerful message to the church about the key role it can play in promoting adoption. This is a wonderful book in which Russell very effectively weaves in mankind's own story of adoption by God. The personal accounts are particularly moving. To be pro-life, you have to be pro-adoption."

> —CHUCK COLSON, Founder, Prison Fellowship

"The older I grow, the more I am personally convinced that the church is our Lord's answer to the adopting of so many precious children who so desperately are in need of a good home. Dr. Russell Moore has done the church a tremendous service by reminding us in this writing of the call of God to meet the ever pressing needs of these little ones. Read with the intent to obey."

> —JOHNNY HUNT, President, Southern Baptist Convention

"Russell Moore is a gift of God to the Christian community and a gift of the Christian community to the nation. His writings on questions of the most profound human and moral significance never fail to instruct and inspire. In *Adopted for Life*, Dr. Moore draws on his family's own experience with adoption to help others understand that by adopting orphaned or abandoned children we can grow in love of God and neighbor and come to appreciate more deeply our own adoption into the family of God through the life, teaching, death, and resurrection of Jesus."
> —ROBERT P. GEORGE, McCormick Professor of Jurisprudence and
> Director of the James Madison Program in American Ideals
> and Institutions, Princeton University

"*Adopted for Life* is truly an incredible book of hope in so many ways. I know of no other book that is so biblically rich, so very practical, and so authentic and heart-felt about the beautiful gift of adoption as this one. It a powerfully insightful book of how adoption is a beautiful act of love and mission for the gospel. I pray that God uses this book to encourage and impact many, many lives."
> —DAN KIMBALL, author of *They Like Jesus but Not the Church*

"Russell Moore has out of personal experience and with biblical accuracy produced in this work an understanding of God's purposes in adoption and its connection with gospel compassion. Every pastor should consider the responsibility he has in making adoption a priority for the church as a viable representation of the gospel doctrine of adoption."
> —JOHN MACARTHUR, Pastor, Grace Community Church,
> Sun Valley, California

"Thankfully, there are good books on adoption and good books on the gospel. But until the arrival of *Adopted for Life*, there has never been a book that puts the adoption of children so clearly within the context of the gospel of Christ. *Adopted for Life* is one of the most compelling books I have ever read—both deeply touching and richly theological. You will never look at adoption or the gospel in quite the same way after reading this book. How could the church have been missing this for so long?"
> —R. ALBERT MOHLER JR., President, The Southern Baptist
> Theological Seminary

"*Adopted for Life* is the fruit of deeply felt personal experience shaped by prolonged theological reflection. Without by any means answering every question we might raise, Russell Moore invites readers to learn to think of adoption in the light of Christian faith. This is a book not only for those who have adopted, those who may adopt, or those who have been adopted, but for all who know themselves to have been freely adopted by God's grace."
> —GILBERT MEILAENDER, Duesenberg Professor in Christian Ethics
> Valparaiso University

"*Adopted for Life* is a well-written rooting of adoption in biblical theology. Moore, who weaves in the story of the two Russian children he and his wife have adopted, shows how churches should view adoption as part of their mission. He shows what a difference it would make if Christians were known once again as the people who take in orphans and make them sons and daughters."

> —MARVIN OLASKY, Editor-in-chief, *World*; Provost, The King's College, New York City

"Yes, yes, yes! Russell Moore has given the church a God-centered, gospel-saturated, culturally-sensitive, mission-focused, desperately needed exploration of the priority and privilege of adoption. He exposes misconceptions and uncovers misunderstandings that not only keep us from fostering an adoptive culture in our churches but that keep us from truly understanding the gospel by which we are adopted as sons and daughters of God. This book contains encouragement for children who have been adopted and the parents who've adopted them, practical advice for parents who are considering adoption and parents who have never considered adoption, and admonishment for the church-at-large to consider how to be obedient to scriptural commands to care for orphans here and around the world. Readers will find themselves laughing on one page, crying on the next, and ultimately bowing before God, thanking him for adopting them into his heavenly family and considering how to show his love to the fatherless on earth."

> —DAVID PLATT, Pastor, The Church at Brook Hills, Birmingham, Alabama

"It is a remarkable story of how two parents chose and adopted two sons from the squalor of a Russian orphanage. It is a remarkable story of how a loving God chose and adopted us from the filth and squalor of sin. It is the remarkable story of an earthly father who lays his hands on the heads of his four sons each evening and prays for their salvation, for their godliness, courage, and conviction, and for them to be given godly wives. It is the remarkable story of a Heavenly Father who loves us so much that he gave his own Son to die for us. Anyone who has adopted, who is considering adoption, or who has been adopted should read Russell Moore's *Adopted for Life*. And anyone who wants to a get a glimpse of the greatness of the Father's love for him or her should read it as well."

> —THOM S. RAINER, President and CEO, LifeWay Christian Resources

"Russell Moore helps all believers, through his very honest, transparent, and theologically enriched book, to see the gospel and reality of Christ through a very fresh lens called adoption. God is working to bring revival and revolution to his church through orphan ministry, and this book is a must for those who will receive his invitation to consider a fatherless child or simply love them through missions."

> —PAUL PENNINGTON, Executive Director, Hope for Orphans

"The care and honesty that Russell Moore demonstrates throughout *Adopted for Life* should inspire every believer to consider God's heart for children without a family. It is adoption that demonstrates our Heavenly Father's desire to know us intimately and personally. He could have called us, forgiven us, justified us, and sanctified us without adopting us. Just like a parable of Christ, the adoption of an orphan provides a lost world the powerful picture of God's personal love for his children. The church must take the lead in caring for orphans and at-risk children, so that adoption is once again united with the message of the Christian gospel."

> —MARK TATLOCK, Provost and Senior Vice President,
> The Master's College

"This book is for all who have been adopted by God. With remarkable narrative flow Russell Moore illumines the beauty and wonder of our adoption in Christ and its profound and necessary implications for orphan care and the earthly practice of adoption. If you want to deepen your worship of the God who adopts and who has revealed himself to be a 'Father to the fatherless,' *Adopted for Life* will serve you exceptionally well."

> —DAN CRUVER, Director of Together for Adoption

"The Bible tells us that pure religion is caring for widows and orphans. Dr. Russell Moore challenges Christians to an aspect of Christ's Lordship that many have never considered. His remarkable way of putting our salvation into the context of being adopted into God's family brings a new perspective on being the recipient of undeserved mercy and grace. The author graphically parallels this beautiful spiritual truth with the analogy of his own adopting of two Russian orphans. Understanding what we have all experienced and reading this poignant testimony made me feel compelled to want to adopt every orphan and abused child in the world. Such an idea is not so far-fetched as *Adopted for Life* reminds us of our mission in a lost world waiting to be adopted."

> —JERRY RANKIN, President, International Mission Board of the
> Southern Baptist Convention

ADOPTED FOR LIFE

Also by Russell D. Moore
The Kingdom of Christ:
The New Evangelical Perspective

ADOPTED FOR LIFE

The Priority of Adoption
for Christian Families and Churches

RUSSELL D. MOORE

Foreword by C. J. Mahaney

CROSSWAY

WHEATON, ILLINOIS

Adopted for Life

Copyright © 2009 by Russell D. Moore

Published by Crossway
    1300 Crescent Street
    Wheaton, Illinois 60187

Cover design: Amy Bristow

Cover photo: iStock & Veer

First printing, 2009

Printed in the United States of America

Unless otherwise indicated, Scripture quotations are taken from the ESV® Bible (*The Holy Bible: English Standard Version®*). Copyright © 2001 by Crossway. Used by permission. All rights reserved.

Scripture quotations marked KJV are from the King James Version of the Bible.

ISBN: 978-1-58134-911-5

ISBN PDF: 978-1-4335-0697-0

ISBN Mobipocket: 978-1-4335-0698-7

Library of Congress Cataloging-in-Publication Data
Moore, Russell, 1971–
 Adopted for life : the priority of adoption for Christian families and churches / Russell D. Moore.
  p. cm.
 Includes index.
 ISBN-13: 978-1-58134-911-5 (tpb)
 1. Adoption—Religious aspects—Christianity. I. Title.
HV875.26.M66 2009
248.8'44—dc22   2008055362

Crossway is a publishing ministry of Good News Publishers.

VP		21	20	19	18	17	16	15	14	13	12	11
19	18	17	16	15	14	13	12	11	10	9	8	7

To Benjamin and Timothy,
of course.

You are my beloved sons,
and with you I am well pleased.

Contents

Foreword

I WAS ADOPTED when I was eighteen years old. I wasn't an orphan, the way most people think of that term. I wasn't an abandoned child. But I was in a condition far more serious: I was a stranger to the family of God, a slave to sin, and an object of the justified wrath of God.

And I didn't even realize it until my friend Bob began to share with me the good news that Christ died for my sins. As I listened, God opened my heart to understand and believe the gospel. I turned from my sin and trusted in Jesus Christ's sacrificial death for my sins. In that moment, I was adopted into a new family. God the righteous Judge became my merciful Father.

And if you are a Christian, if you have trusted in Christ's substitutionary sacrifice on the cross for your sins, you too have been adopted.

It would have been extraordinary enough for God simply to redeem us, to forgive our sins, to declare us righteous. But he does not stop here—he makes us his children (Gal. 4:4–7). Christian, if you have ever wondered whether God loves you, wonder no longer. God the Father has adopted you as his son or daughter through the person and work of Christ. Here you will find the richest proof of God's personal, particular, and passionate love for you.

I was reminded of my own adoption many times during the twenty-seven years that I had the privilege to serve as a pastor at Covenant Life Church. Covenant Life is filled with parents who traveled to distant (and sometimes dangerous) countries to adopt a child or who adopted a child in the U.S. Meeting these newly adopted children was a unique joy for me. Each time I felt God's presence. Each time I admired the adoptive parents' selflessness and compassion. Each time I was reminded of the Savior's death for my sins so that I might be adopted by God the Father. Each time I was reminded of God's love for us, displayed in the gospel.

And I had a similar experience when I first read Russell Moore's story of adopting two boys from Russia. A mutual friend sent me the magazine article in which Russell first shared it, and it deeply affected me. I admired Russell and Maria's compassion and love for these children, their selfless willingness to travel such a distance to adopt these boys, their eagerness to welcome Benjamin and Timothy into their family. Even more than that, every time I read their story, I am poignantly reminded of God's love for his adopted children.

I've introduced many others to the Moores' story, and I've personally re-read it several times, but I've never read it in private or in public without tears. I don't think you can read this book without being moved. In fact, before you turn to the first chapter, you should make sure tissues are close by (or if you're a guy, get ready to use your shirtsleeve).

I am so grateful that my friend Russell has written the book you hold in your hands. I want many more people to read this story, to be amazed at God's love displayed in the doctrine of adoption, and to consider the possibility of adopting children themselves. You may not agree with all of Russell's conclusions, but his book will challenge you to carefully consider both the doctrine of adoption and its implications for your life.

So I commend to you my friend Russell Moore's example, and his book. In these pages you will not only encounter one couple's adoption of two Russian children; you will encounter your own adoption. May we all become freshly aware of the adopting grace of God toward undeserving sinners like us.

C. J. Mahaney
Sovereign Grace Ministries

1

Adoption, Jesus, and You

*Why You Should Read This Book, Especially
If You Don't Want to*

MY SONS HAVE A CERTAIN LOOK in their eyes when they are conspiring to do something wrong. They have another, similar look when they are trying to read my face to see if *I* think what they're doing is something wrong. It was this second look I could see buzzing across both of their faces as they walked up the steps to the old pulpit.

My boys were at a chapel service on the campus where I serve to train pastors for Christian ministry; they were there to hear me preach. They know better than to misbehave in church, and this seemed kind of like a church service. They also knew that I had warned them they could only sit up on the front row if they were still and quiet, with nothing distracting going on down there while I was preaching. But a friend of mine had other plans for them that day.

"Benjamin and Timothy," he had whispered only a few minutes earlier to my sons, "will you help me introduce your daddy before he preaches?" I fidgeted with my uncomfortable over-the-ear microphone while I watched these two strong, vibrant, little five-year-old boys walk up the platform steps. They were peering at me the whole time to make sure they weren't breaking the rules that we'd agreed upon. I watched them stand behind the pulpit and listened to them answer questions from my colleague. "Who is going to preach today?" my friend asked. "Daddy," Benjamin responded. "And what's he going to preach about?" he continued. Timothy answered quickly, leaning into the microphone, "Jesus."

For a couple of seconds, my mind flashed back to the first time I ever saw these two boys. They were lying in excrement and vomit, covered in heat blisters and flies, in an orphanage somewhere in a little mining community in Russia. Maria and I had applied to adopt and had gone on the first of two trips, not knowing who, if anyone, we would find waiting for us. Immediately upon landing in the former Soviet Union, I wondered if we had made the worst mistake of our lives.

Sitting in a foreign airport, with the smell of European perfume, human sweat, and cigarette smoke wafting all around us, Maria and I recommitted to God that we would trust him and that we would adopt whomever he directed us to, regardless of what medical or emotional problems they may have. A Russian judge told us she had two "gray-eyed" boys picked out for us, both of whom had been abandoned by their mothers to a hospital in the little village about an hour from where we were staying.

Sure enough, the orphanage authorities, through our translators, cataloged a terrifying list of medical problems, including fetal alcohol syndrome for one, if not both, of the boys. We looked at each other, as if to say, "This is what the Lord has for us, so here we go." The nurse led us up some stairs, down a dank hallway, and into a tiny room with two beds. I can still see the younger of the two, now Timothy, rocking up and down against the bars of his crib, grinning widely. The older, now Benjamin, was more reserved, stroking my five o'clock shadow with his hand and seeing (I came to realize) a man most probably for the very first time in his life. Both the boys had hair matted down on their heads, and one of them had crossed eyes. Both of them moved slowly and rigidly, almost like stop-motion clay animated characters from the Christmas television specials of our 1970s childhoods. And we loved them both, at an intuitive and almost primal level, from the very first second.

The transformation of these two ex-orphans into the sons I

saw behind the pulpit that day and see every day of my life running through my house with Lego toys and construction paper drawings motivates me to write this book. The thought that there are thousands more like them in orphanages in Russia, in government facilities in China, and in foster care systems in the United States haunts me enough to sit at this computer and type.

I don't know who you are, reading this book. Maybe you're standing in a bookstore, flipping past these pages. Maybe you're reading this book a few minutes at a time, keeping it in a drawer so your spouse won't see it. Maybe you never thought you'd read a book about adoption. Maybe you're wondering if you should.

Well, okay. I never thought I'd write a book about adoption, as you'll see soon enough. Like I said, I don't know who you are. But I know that I am writing this to you. I invite you to spend the next little bit thinking with me about a subject that has everything to do with you, whoever you are.

Whenever I told people I was working on a book on adoption, they'd often say something along the lines of, "Great. So, is the book about the doctrine of adoption or, you know, real adoption?" That's a hard question to answer because you can't talk about the one without talking about the other. Also, it is not as though we master one aspect and then move to the other—from the vertical to the horizontal or the other way around. That's not the picture God has embedded in his creation work.

The Bible tells us that human families are reflective of an eternal fatherhood (Eph. 3:14–15). We know, then, what human fatherhood ought to look like on the basis of how our Father God behaves toward us. But the reverse is also true. We see something of the way our God is fatherly toward us through our relationships with human fathers. And so Jesus tells us that in our human father's provision and discipline we get a glimpse of God's active love for us (Matt. 7:9–11; cf. Heb. 12:5–17). The same truth is at work in adoption.

Adoption is, on the one hand, *gospel*. In this, adoption tells us who we are as children of the Father. Adoption as gospel tells us about our identity, our inheritance, and our mission as sons of God. Adoption is also defined as *mission*. In this, adoption tells us our purpose in this age as the people of Christ. Missional adoption spurs us to join Christ in advocating for the helpless and the abandoned.

As soon as you peer into the truth of the one aspect, you fall headlong into the truth of the other, and vice versa. That's because it's the way the gospel is. Jesus reconciles us to God and to each other. As we love our God, we love our neighbor; as we love our neighbor, we love our God. We believe Jesus in heavenly things—our adoption in Christ; so we follow him in earthly things—the adoption of children. Without the theological aspect, the emphasis on adoption too easily is seen as mere charity. Without the missional aspect, the doctrine of adoption too easily is seen as mere metaphor.

But adoption is contested, both in its cosmic and missional aspects. The Scriptures tell us there are unseen beings in the air around us who would rather we not think about what it means to be who we are in Christ. These rulers of this age would rather we ignore both the eternal reality and the earthly icon of it. They would rather we find our identity, our inheritance, and our mission according to what we can see and verify as ours—according to what the Bible calls "the flesh"—rather than according to the veiled rhythms of the Spirit of life. That's why adoption isn't charity—it's war.

The gospel of Jesus Christ means our families and churches ought to be at the forefront of the adoption of orphans close to home and around the world. As we become more attuned to the gospel, we'll have more of a burden for orphans. As we become more adoption-friendly, we'll be better able to understand the gospel. This book calls us to look forward to an adoptive-missional church. In this book I want to call us all to consider how encouraging adoption—whether we adopt or whether we help others adopt—can help us peer into the ancient mystery of our faith in Christ and can help us restore the fracturing unity and the atrophied mission of our congregations.

It is one thing when the culture doesn't "get" adoption. What else could one expect when all of life is seen as the quest of "selfish genes" for survival? It is one thing when the culture doesn't "get" adoption and so speaks of buying a cat as "adopting" a pet. But when those who follow Christ think the same way, we betray that we miss something crucial about our own salvation.

Adoption is not just about couples who want children—or who want more children. Adoption is about an entire culture within our churches, a culture that sees adoption as part of our Great Commission mandate and as a sign of the gospel itself. This book is intended for families who want to adopt and wonder whether they should. It is also intended for parents with children who've been adopted and who wonder how to raise them from here. It is for middle-aged fathers and mothers whose children have just told them they are thinking about adoption.

But this book is also, and perhaps most especially, for the man who flinches when his wife raises the issue of adoption because he wants his "own kids"—and who hates himself a little for thinking like that. It is for the wife who keeps the adoption application papers in a pile on the exercise bicycle upstairs—as a "last resort"—but who is praying fervently right now for two lines of purple to show up on her home pregnancy test. It is for the single twenty-something who assumes that he will marry after a couple of years in the post-college job force, find a nice girl, have a honeymoon for three or four years, and then they'll start thinking about getting pregnant. It is for the pastor who preaches about adoption as an alternative to abortion on a Sanctity of Human Life Sunday but who has never considered how to envision for his congregation what it would mean to see family after family after family in the church directory in which the children bear little physical resemblance to, and maybe even don't share the skin color of, their parents. It is for the elderly couple who tithe their Social Security check, dote on their grandchildren, and wonder how they can tangibly help the young couple who ask for prayer every month that they might be parents—and who never seem to show up for Mother's Day services.

Before we begin, though, let me tell you what this book is *not*. It is not a step-by-step guide to navigating the adoption process, complete with legal advice and agency recommendations. There are good resources available on those things. Second, even if I set out to write a book like that, the whirl of change in this area is such that it would probably be out-of-date by the time you read it. In the United States, state laws change sometimes month to month. Around the world countries authorize international adoption and then close down, only to reopen later. Those logistical issues are much easier than you think. Finding out the reputation and competency of an adoption agency, whether Christian or secular, is not much more complicated than a Google search. And the process itself is mapped out, in as much detail as possible, by a good agency.

Instead I want to ask what it would mean if our churches and families were known as the people who adopt babies—and toddlers, and children, and teenagers. What if we as Christians were known, once again, as the people who take in orphans and make of them beloved sons and daughters?

Not everyone is called to adopt. No one wants parents who adopt children out of the same sense of duty with which they may give to the building fund for the new church gymnasium. But all of us have a stake in the adoption issue, because Jesus does. He is the one who tells us his Father is also "Father of the fatherless" (Ps. 68:5). He is the one who insists on calling "the least of these" his "brothers" (Matt. 25:40) and who tells us that the first time we hear his voice, he will be asking us if we did the same.

I don't know why, in the mystery of God's plan, you were led to pick up this book. But I know this: you have a stake in the adoption issue, even if you never adopt a child. There's a war going on around you—and perhaps within you—and adoption is one crucial arena of that war. With that in mind, there are perhaps some changes to be made in our lives. For some of us, I hope this book changes the makeup of our households. For some of us, I hope it helps change our monthly bank account balances. For all of us, I hope it changes something of the way we say "brother" and "sister" in our pews next Sunday and the way we cry out "Father" on our knees tonight.

This book is less about a dogmatic set of assertions (although there are some of those) than it is a conversation with you about what I have seen and what I've been taught through adoption and what I hope we can all learn together.

And as we start this conversation together, I can't help but think again of the image of my sons standing behind that pulpit. I'll admit I was proud of them that day, as I am every day. I don't idealize them. They are sinners, like all of us. They deserve to be in hell forever, like all of us. And sometimes they are selfish, whining brats—just like their dad.

That day in that chapel, though, I managed to forget about my fatherly pride for a few minutes—and certainly to forget about adoption and orphanages and the events that led to our becoming parents. I just stood up and preached. When I finished, prayed, and walked down the steps from the pulpit, one of my sons, Benjamin, stepped out to the front of the chapel to shake my hand. Where did this little man come from, who stood with such dignity to tell his daddy he loved him and was proud of him? That probably didn't seem to anyone in the room like an act of warfare—but, oh, how it was.

As I knelt down and hugged him, I realized how small and shallow and needy I had been when, only a few years ago, I had refused to go with my wife to an adoption seminar. I'd been "too busy" to go. "My life's a whirlwind right now, you know," I'd said to her at the time. But, really, the idea of adoption left me cold. Now, I was pro-adoption, of course, as a social and political matter (hadn't I been saying that in my pro-life writings and speeches for years?). But why couldn't we wait and exhaust all the ethically appropriate reproductive technologies before thinking about adoption? I told my wife, "I don't mind adopting a few years down the road, but I want my first child to be *mine*." I can still hear my voice saying those words—and it sounds so small and pitiable and hellish now.

How could I have known what it was like to hold this little boy in my arms, and his brother with him, knit together with them by a fatherhood that surpassed my genetic code? How could I have read and preached and lectured on Ephesians and Galatians and Romans, how could I have lectured through classroom notes on the doctrine of adoption, without ever seeing *this*? I wasn't evil—or, at least, I wasn't any more evil on this score than any other redeemed sinner— but I was as theologically and spiritually vacuous as the television "prosperity gospel" preachers I made fun of with my theologically sophisticated friends.

Some of you are in the place where I was several years ago. Some of you are where I am now. Some of you are where I will be, by God's grace, when I pronounce one of my sons husband to a godly woman or when I hug one of them as he receives his high-school diploma or, best of all, when I baptize one of them as my brother in Christ.

This book isn't, first of all, a theological treatise on adoption in the abstract, although I hope it helps some of us to see how adoption pictures something true about our God and his ways. This book isn't primarily a book about the practical joys and challenges of adopting children, although I hope it helps many more moms and dads to know firsthand something of why I am wiping away tears as I type this right now. Ultimately, this book isn't really about adoption at all. It's just what my son Timothy probably would tell you it is about, if you asked him. It's about Jesus.

2

Are They Brothers?

*What Some Rude Questions about Adoption Taught Me
about the Gospel of Christ*

SO, ARE THEY BROTHERS?" the woman asked. My wife
Maria and I, jet-lagged from just returning from Russia, looked at
each other wearily. This was the twelfth time since we returned that
we'd been asked this question. When I looked back at the woman's
face, she had her eyebrows raised. "Are they?" she repeated. "Are
they brothers?"

This lady was looking at some pictures, printed off a computer,
of two one-year-old boys in a Russian orphanage, boys who had
only days earlier been pronounced by a Russian court to be our children, after the legally mandated waiting period had elapsed for the
paperwork to go through. Maria and I had returned to Kentucky to
wait for the call to return to pick up our children and had only these
pictures of young Maxim and Sergei, our equivalent of a prenatal
sonogram, to show to our friends and relatives back home. But
people kept asking, "Are they brothers?"

"They are now," I replied. "Yes," the woman said. "I know.
But are they *really* brothers?" Clenching my jaw, and repeating
Beatitudes to myself silently in my mind, I coolly responded, "Yes,
now they are both our children, so they are now *really* brothers."
The woman sighed, rolled her eyes, and said, "Well, you know what
I mean."

Of course, we did know what she meant. What she wondered
was whether these two boys, born three weeks apart, share a com-

mon biological ancestry, a common bloodline, some common DNA. It struck me that this question betrayed what most of us tend to view as *really* important when it comes to sonship: traceable genetic material.

This is the reason people would also ask us, "Now, do you have any children of your own?" And it is the reason newspaper obituaries will often refer to the deceased's "adopted child," as though this were the equivalent of a stepchild or a protégé rather than a *real* offspring.

During the weeks that Maria and I waited anxiously for the call to return to Russia to receive our children, I pondered this series of questions. As I read through the books of Ephesians and Galatians and Romans, it occurred to me that this is precisely the question that was faced by the apostle Paul and the first-century Christian churches.

As pig-flesh-eating Gentile believers—formerly goddess worshipers and Caesar-magnifiers and all the rest—began confessing Jesus as the Messiah, some Jewish Christians demanded to know, "Are they circumcised?" This meant, of course, "Are they really part of us? Are they our brothers?" The Gentile believers would respond, "Yes, with the circumcision made without hands, the circumcision of Christ." From the heated letters of the New Testament, it's evident that the response to that was along the lines of, "Yes, but are you *really* circumcised . . . and you know what I mean."

This was no peripheral issue. For the apostle Paul, the unity of the church as a household has everything to do with the gospel itself. And where the tribal fracturing of the church is most threatening, Paul lays out a key insight into the church's union with Christ—the Spirit of adoption. For Paul, adoption isn't simply one more literary image to convey "Jesus in my heart." It has everything to do with our identity and our inheritance in Christ, with who we are and where we're headed.

Maria and I went to Russia and back, twice, to accomplish a task, to complete a long paper trail that would bring us to the legal custody of our sons. Along with that, however, it jolted us with the truth of an adoption more ancient, more veiled, but just as real: our own.

OUR ADOPTED IDENTITY

When Maria and I first walked into the orphanage, where we were led to the boys the Russian courts had picked out for us to adopt, we almost vomited in reaction to the stench and squalor of the place. The boys were in cribs, in the dark, lying in their own waste.

Leaving them at the end of each day was painful, but leaving them the final day, before going home to wait for the paperwork to go through, was the hardest thing either of us had ever done. Walking out of the room to prepare for the plane ride home, Maria and I could hear Maxim calling out for us and falling down in his crib, convulsing in tears. Maria shook with tears of her own. I turned around to walk back into their room, just for a minute.

I placed my hand on both of their heads and said, knowing they couldn't understand a word of English, "I will not leave you as orphans; I will come to you." I don't think I consciously intended to cite Jesus' words to his disciples in John 14:18; it just seemed like the only thing worth saying at the time.

For us, it didn't matter that they seemed like any other orphan in that institution; they were part of our family now. We knew them. We loved them. We claimed them. And it didn't matter that for the next several weeks they'd still be called "Maxim" and "Sergei." The nameplates hanging on the wall of their new room in a faraway country read "Benjamin" and "Timothy."

In one sense, my sons' situation was quite unique. In another sense, though, their lives marked from the very beginning the kind of ambiguity that often comes along with adoption. Sometimes people will speak of children who've been adopted as prone to having an "identity crisis" at some point in their lives. This isn't the case for every child, of course, but it does seem that many children who were adopted find themselves asking at some point, "Who am I?" The

Bible reveals, though, that this kind of crisis of identity isn't limited to children who've been adopted. All of us are looking to discover who we really are, whether we were born into loving homes or abandoned at orphanage doors, whether we were born into stable families or born, like our Lord, in a stable.

I guess that's what bothered me so much about the "are they brothers?" question. There was almost a note of implied pity—as though, if they were biologically brothers, well, then at least they'd have each other. The query seemed to be asking, "Is this a real family or just a legal fiction?" The question seemed to render them orphans again.

That question isn't new.

In his letter to the church at Rome, the apostle Paul raises the issue of adoption, just as he does in similar letters to the churches at Galatia and Ephesus. But before he begins his discussion, he addresses the assembled congregation as "brothers" (Rom. 8:12). That's a word that's lost its meaning in our churches, I fear. We tend to view it as a mere spiritual metaphor for "friend" or "acquaintance." Perhaps in your church, "brother" is a safe word you might use when you've forgotten someone's name ("Hey, brother, how are you?") or to soften some hurtful comment ("I can't marry you, Johnny, but I love you . . . as a brother in Christ").

The churches emerging out of Judaism in the first century, however, would have understood precisely how radical this "brothers" language is. The "sons of Israel" started out, after all, not as a government entity but as twelve brothers. Everywhere in the Old Testament the people of Israel are defined as "brothers" as opposed to "strangers" or "sojourners" (for example, Lev. 25:35–46 and Deut. 17:15). That's why Jesus' hearers can't get his references to "loving your neighbor" in his story about a Good Samaritan (Luke 10:27, 29). Their Bibles clearly refer to a "neighbor" as one's fellow Israelite, a kinsman by blood, one of one's people, one's brother (Lev. 19:17–18).

It's hard for us to get the force of the "brothers" language since almost none of us think of ourselves as "Gentiles." That's a safe, boring "Bible word." We would never claim our identity around something as, well, private as whether we've been circumcised. We might think of ourselves as American or Australian, blue-collar or white-collar, Republican or Democrat, or any number of other things, but words like "Gentile" or "uncircumcised" seem very distant from our lives.

Imagine, though, that you live in a very different age, a land without electric lights or telecommunication. You've never been more than ten miles from your home. Your family doesn't talk to you anymore, and you've lost your job. You got caught up in this foreign cult, one that teaches that this executed insurrectionist has come back from the dead. You'll never forget your mother's face when she asked you if it was true that you and your new friends eat human skin and drink human blood together in your meetings. You've walked away from all you've ever known.

And yet when you arrive at the house, with the rest of your fellow Messiah-followers, things get uncomfortable for you, again. One of the pastors reads those old words, from one of the books of Moses. It talks about how "the uncircumcised" are "cut off" from the promises of God. You squirm a little bit in your seat. You know, should anyone bother to check, that you'd never pass for circumcised. No one's ever offered to make the cut for you, and you kind of hope they don't.

As a matter of fact, the more you think about it, every time people like you are mentioned in the book you believe is the Word of your God, it seems to always be pointing out that you're "the other." Sure, sometimes people like you are spoken of as "strangers and aliens" to be treated well. But most of the time you're one of the villains of the story, with names like Goliath, Nebuchadnezzar, or Jezebel. People like you keep getting their heads cut off by the good guys in the story, or else they're drowned by God himself. You're what they call a "Gentile." And your only hope in the world is a Jewish king, one nobody's heard from in years and one that most of the Jews themselves don't even recognize as the real thing.

If this were the scenario today, I can only imagine the way we'd de-emphasize those uncomfortable Old Testament texts in our public reading of Scripture, our preaching, our worship songs. I can imagine the kind of "recovering Philistines" support groups we might have if the gospel had first shown up in our culture rather than theirs. But the New Testament does no such thing. The apostolic gospel deals with the sordid past of the Gentiles who now claim Christ as their own, and it does so with jarring honesty.

These Gentiles are reminded that they are, by nature, pagans. Their background is a story of rebels turning from the God of creation to worshipping trees, rocks, and snakes and to carrying out all their twisted cravings (Rom. 1:16–2:16). They were "alienated from the commonwealth of Israel and strangers to the covenants of promise, having no hope and without God in the world" (Eph. 2:12). They followed after the demonic powers, "carrying out the desires of the body and the mind" (Eph. 2:3). They were "enslaved to those that by nature are not gods" (Gal. 4:8).

This must have seemed to some of the new Christ-followers like your friend who reminds you every week that, yes, he's the one who found you your current job and, why, yes, he's the one who loaned you the money to pay for your college education and—yes, now that you mention it—he's the one who introduced you to your spouse. I imagine if I had been in one of the earlier congregations, listening to these letters read to me, I might have been thinking something like, "If my old life is 'crucified' with Jesus, then why should I remember it? If the Gentiles are 'children of promise' right along with the Jews, then why do you have to keep reminding us we're Gentiles? If 'neither circumcision counts for anything, nor uncircumcision' (Gal. 6:15), then why do you keep bringing it up?"

But the flight from one's old identity is part of the gospel itself. That's what repentance is, which is why the adoption passages of the New Testament spend so much time warning against finding one's identity in "the flesh." Now, "the flesh," for Paul, isn't the body. It is instead one's creaturely aspect considered apart from the direction of

God's Spirit. It's the old order, that old pattern of confidence in one's self, the refusal to see oneself as a creature in need of lordship. That's ultimately a question of identity. Am I the sum total of my biological background, of my biological urges, or of the markings made in my skin by my parents?

This question of identity is why Paul warns so strongly about "walking according to the flesh" rather than the Spirit, about returning to patterns that were left behind. One's "flesh" shows who one's father is—and that's terrifying. When we "bite and devour one another" (Gal. 5:15), we're imaging one who seeks "someone to devour" (1 Pet. 5:8), not the One who came to seek and save that which was lost.

Imagine for a moment that you're adopting a child. As you meet with the social worker in the last stage of the process, you're told that this twelve-year-old has been in and out of psychotherapy since he was three. He persists in burning things and attempting repeatedly to skin kittens alive. He "acts out sexually," the social worker says, although she doesn't really fill you in on what that means. She continues with a little family history. This boy's father, grandfather, great-grandfather, and great-great-grandfather all had histories of violence, ranging from spousal abuse to serial murder. Each of them ended life the same way, death by suicide—each found hanging from a rope of blankets in his respective prison cell.

Think for a minute. Would you want this child? If you did adopt him, wouldn't you keep your eye on him as he played with your other children? Would you watch him nervously as he looks at the butcher knife on the kitchen table? Would you leave the room as he watched a movie on television with your daughter, with the lights out?

Well, he's you. And he's me. That's what the gospel is telling us. Our birth father has fangs. And left to ourselves, we'll show ourselves to be as serpentine as he is.

That's why our sin ought to disturb us. The "works of the flesh"—jealousy, envy, wrath, lust, hatred, and on and on—ought to alarm us the way a tightness in the chest would alarm a man whose father and grandfather had dropped dead at the age of forty of heart disease. It ought to scare us like forgetting the next-door neighbor's name would scare a woman whose mother was institutionalized on her thirty-fifth birthday for dementia. It's easy to deceive ourselves though. The chest pains? They're just indigestion. The forgetfulness? It's just because of a hectic schedule. Even this self-deceit shows us our similarity to our reptilian birth father. He, after all, "knows that his time is short" but rages away against God and his Christ anyway (Rev. 12:12).

But the New Testament addresses former Satan-imagers with good news. It's not just that we have a stay of execution, a suspension of doom. It's not simply that those who trust in Christ have found a refuge, a safe place, or a foster home. All those in Christ, Paul argues, have received sonship. We are now "Abraham's offspring" (Gal. 3:29). Within this household—the tribal family of Abraham—all those who are in Christ have found a home through the adopting power of God.

The New Testament reminds those of us who are newcomers of our adoption so we'll remember that we are here by the Spirit, not by the exertions of our flesh. Because we've been brought into an already-existing family, we ought not to be proud, as though we were here by family entitlement (Rom. 11:11–25). We're here by grace.

But our adoption also shows us just how welcome we are here. This is not, after all, the first time, God has adopted. Too often we assume that the Gentiles are the "adopted" children of God, and the Jews are the "natural-born" children. But Paul says that Israel was adopted too (Rom. 9:4). Of Israel, God once said, "Your origin and your birth are of the land of the Canaanites; your father was an Amorite and your mother a Hittite" (Ezek. 16:3). The Israelites were once Gentiles too. God reminds Israel that he "found him in a desert land, and in the howling waste of the wilderness" (Deut. 32:10). Israel was an abandoned baby, wallowing in its own blood on the roadside (Ezek. 16:5).

That's why Paul seems so furious at the idea that Gentiles would be forced to undergo circumcision. Circumcision answers the question, "Are you a part of the family? Are the promises made to you? Are you in the covenant?" The Jewish believers who prize circumcision want to see themselves, and others, apart from Christ. It's a lack of faith, a lack of repentance. If they are clinging to their identity in Christ, being found in him, then everything else is "rubbish" (Phil. 3:8–9). Yes, we're part of the family, but we don't point to our own circumcised flesh to prove that; we point away from ourselves and to a circumcised, law-keeping, faithful, resurrected Messiah (Col. 2:11–13). And the Jewish leaders who insist on circumcision for Gentile believers are looking under the wrong robe.

The promise has dawned, and our identity is now found in him. All of us—whatever our background—have been liberated from the old order (Gal. 4:1–5) and from "the spirit of slavery to fall back into fear" (Rom. 8:15). We now come before God *as sons* bearing the very same Spirit as was poured out on the Lord Jesus at the Jordan River, a Spirit through which we cry, "Abba!"

This means repentance. We recognize and know that we never could have found ourselves in this family "through the flesh"—whether that striving was through biblical circumcision or through pagan orgies or through modern self-absorption. Our identity is found in another—Jesus of Nazareth.

The "are they brothers?" question irritated me so much, the more I thought about it, because it was about more than my adoption process. It was about my pride and self-delusion. It reminded me of my own tendency to prize my carnality, a tendency the Scripture warns leads right to the grave (Rom. 8:13). None of us likes to think we were adopted. We assume we're natural-born children, with a right to all of this grace, to all of this glory.

We think, Paul warns us right before he tells us of our adoption, that we are "debtors . . . to the flesh," so we "live according to the flesh" (Rom. 8:12). We're ashamed to think of ourselves as adopted, because to do so would focus our minds on the gory truth that all of us in Christ, like my sons, once were lost but now we're found, once were strangers and now we're children, once were slaves and now we're heirs.

And yet, even the flesh and blood we share—not just with our children but with all of humanity—has everything to do with our adoption. Jesus, after all, shares in human "flesh and blood" so that he might deliver those who "through fear of death were subject to lifelong slavery" (Heb. 2:14–15). Jesus took on everything—from blushing skin to sweating pores to firing adrenal glands to moving bowels—all because he "had to be made like his brothers in every respect" (Heb. 2:17). And, speaking of us, our Lord Jesus, the only One with the natural-born right to cry, "Abba," "is not ashamed to call them brothers" (Heb. 2:11).

According to the apostle John, the religious leaders of Jesus' day were quite sure of their biological pedigree. They could trace it back to Abraham. If called upon, they could pull up their robes and prove their place in the community with a mark in their skin. They had no shady parental background as they thought Jesus to have (John 8:39–41). Jesus, however, identified their birth father as Satan and their inheritance as that of a slave (John 8:34–38).

But John ends his Gospel with a more hopeful sound. Jesus' first words as a resurrected man weren't about philosophy or theology or predictions about the end of the age. Instead, his first words included a message to Mary to go "to my brothers and say to them, 'I am ascending to my Father and your Father, to my God and your God'" (John 20:17).

Think about these words for a moment. They're being formed by a tongue and teeth that, just hours before, were dead tissue in a hole in the Middle East. If you could catch even a hint of how awe-filled these words are, you'd drop this book right now—and I'd stop typing it—and we'd both fall to our knees in tears.

Remember—these men he calls "brothers" were at that very moment sniveling cowards at best and insurrectionists at worst. They were hiding in a room somewhere, listening for the sound of soldiers' feet. They'd walked away from Christ and him crucified. They were ashamed of the gospel. But he wasn't ashamed of them.

John wasn't "really" Jesus' brother, was he? But he shares a mother with him, in that Jesus "adopts" him into the family at the cross, commissioning him to do what a family member is to do—to care for a mother in distress (John 19:26–27).

And these unfaithful and fearful disciples, quick to go back to the fisherman's nets they had when he found them, had no reason to approach a holy Creator, no reason to call him "our God." But they—and we—are Jesus' brothers, and so the Father is our God. He is not ashamed.

But that's hard to believe.

The New Testament continually points to our adoption in Christ in order to show us that we're really, *really* wanted here in the Father's house. The Spirit is continually telling the people of Christ that they, we, are "blessed" in Christ through adoption (Eph. 1:3, 5). We are all Abraham's children because Jesus is (Gal. 3:28–29). Perhaps we were "at one time" Gentiles, but we aren't part of the uncircumcised order anymore (Eph. 2:11). We are now all "fellow citizens with the saints and members of the household of God" (Eph. 2:19). We are to exchange our "old self" for the "new self, created after the likeness of God" (Eph. 4:22–24). We are now brothers (Rom. 8:12).

The Gentile Christians in the early churches must have wondered what they were doing, following after this Jewish king from somebody else's religion. Had they wandered accidentally into somebody else's covenant? Were they clinging to some kind of "exception clause" to God's main purpose with Israel? Were they parasites on the promises of God?

Some of the Jewish believers, those with consciences sensitive enough to see how uncircumcised their hearts could be too, must have wondered something similar.

Don't you know what that feels like too, to wonder if you're an accidental visitor awkwardly standing in the corner of a party to which you've not been invited? What if our whole lives are like

that? What if we're in the kind of situation described by humorist
Jack Handey when he writes, "The crows seemed to be calling his
name, thought Caw"?[1]

This fear is exactly why the New Testament ties our adoption to
God's purpose in election. We were known beforehand, the Bible says,
predestined "to be conformed to the image of his Son, that he might
be the firstborn among many brothers" (Rom. 8:29). In love, the text
says, "he predestined us for adoption as sons through Jesus Christ"
(Eph. 1:4–5). Paul tells us that we have not only "come to know God"
but rather that we have come "to be known by God" (Gal. 4:9).

Now I realize that the mention of words like *election* and *predestination* are making some of you tense up right now, and I understand why. But it's really not a scary concept. All Christians believe
in election and predestination—these are Bible words, after all.

We sometimes disagree about how God's purpose fits with other
things the Bible reveals—that God loves all people and wants to see
all people come to Christ, that God is impartial, that human beings
make free choices for which they're held personally responsible. We
often have different opinions about the finer points of this mystery,
and we can live together with some tension here.

It's important to know that nothing about the biblical doctrine of
election is meant to cast doubt on whether you're welcome in God's
household. God is not some metaphysical airport security screener,
waving through the secretly pre-approved and sending the rest into a
holding tank for questioning. God isn't treating us like puppets made
of meat, forcing us along by his capricious whim.

Instead, the doctrine of election tells us that all of us who have
come to know Christ are here on purpose. God was looking for us.
He rejoices in us. And he cries out, "I was ready to be sought by those
who did not ask for me; I was ready to be found by those who did
not seek me. I said, 'Here am I, here am I,' to a nation that was not
called by my name" (Isa. 65:1). That's all of us, you and me. There's
freedom in that, and a liberating sense of belonging.

---

[1]Jack Handey, *Deeper Thoughts* (New York: Hyperion, 1993), 13.

How do you know if you're part of this household? The Spirit of God is there.

The Spirit, after all, is the One in the Old Testament who marks out who the king is, the anointed one, called by God his "son." That's how you know that David is king and Saul isn't anymore. It's not by the royal entourage or the title or the office. Saul has all of these for a long time after he's rejected as king. It's the presence of the Spirit on David, a Spirit who empowers him to behead giants and sing songs of praise (1 Sam. 16–30). The Spirit also marks out who Israel is, the children of promise, raising them from the dead and announcing them as the heirs of God (Ezek. 37:13–14).

When "the flesh" can't reproduce a deliverer for the human race, the Spirit overshadows a virgin's uterus and conceives a new humanity (Luke 1:35). The Spirit descends on Jesus at his baptism, as God's voice proclaims his acceptance of his "beloved Son" (Matt. 3:17). When Jesus is raised from the dead by the power of the Spirit, God declares him "to be the Son of God in power" (Rom. 1:4). If you're united to Christ, then that same Spirit now rests on you (1 Pet. 4:14). You share in his anointing (1 John 2:20, 26–27). To have the Spirit doesn't necessarily mean that you "feel" especially spiritual. It just means you agree with God that Jesus is Lord and that that's good news (1 Cor. 12:3). And it means you agree with Jesus that our Father is in heaven and we can trust him (Matt. 6:9).

"The Spirit himself," Paul tells the Romans, "bears witness with our spirit that we are children of God" (Rom. 8:16). This isn't some giddy, emotional experience—a comforting whisper in our consciences that we're of Christ. The Spirit simply points us to Jesus and identifies us with him. Because we share the Spirit with Jesus, we cry out with him to the same Father (Rom. 8:15; Gal. 4:6). And since what unites us to Jesus is his Spirit, not our flesh, we share a common family with all those who also have this Spirit resting upon them. Since there's one Spirit, there's "one Lord, one faith, one baptism, one God and Father of all" (Eph. 4:5–6).

That's adoption. We're part of a brand-new family, a new tribe, with a new story, a new identity.

As Maria and I went through the adoption process, we were encouraged by everyone from social workers to family friends to "teach the children about their cultural heritage." We have done just that.

Now, what most people probably meant by this counsel is for us to teach our boys Russian folk tales and Russian songs, observing Russian holidays, and so forth. But as we see it, that's not their heritage anymore, and we hardly want to signal to them that they are strangers and aliens, even welcome ones, in our home. We teach them about their heritage, yes, but their heritage as Mississippians. They hear, then, about their great-grandfather, a faithful Baptist pastor from Tippah County. I tell them how the deacons at his church would give his paycheck to my grandmother because they were afraid he'd give it all away to the poor in his flock. They learn about their great-great-grandfather who worked hard raising cotton but couldn't overcome his drinking. They learn about their people before them in the Confederate army and the civil rights movement.

Yes, I'll read Dostoyevsky and Tolstoy to them one day, I suppose, but not with the same intensity with which I'll read to them William Faulkner and Eudora Welty. They wouldn't know an arrangement of "Peter and the Wolf" if they heard it, but they can recognize the voices of Charley Pride and Hank Williams in seconds. When we sit at the table for our holiday meals, they don't eat borscht. They eat what we eat—red beans and rice or fried catfish or shrimp risotto. They share our lives, and our story. They belong here. They are Moores now, with all that entails.

I suppose this is why the New Testament so repeatedly points all of us toward the Old Testament narratives, which are given, as Paul tells the church at Corinth, "as examples for us" (1 Cor. 10:6). It's not just that these accounts show us something universal about human nature and God's workings. It is that they are our story, our heritage, our identity.

Those are our ancestors rescued from Egypt, wandering in the wilderness, led back from exile. They are our forefathers, and this is our family. Whether our background is Norwegian or Haitian or Indonesian, if we are united to Christ, our family genealogy is found not primarily in the front pages of our dusty old family Bible but inside its pages, in the first chapter of the Gospel of Matthew. Our identity is in Christ; so his people are our people, his God our God.

We know the first Christians were persecuted. What we don't think about often is how lonely many of them must have been. Many of them would have been told by their parents, their siblings, their spouses, and their villages not to speak to them again until they pulled themselves out of this fishermen's cult. The Spirit of adoption didn't just wrench them away from their family ties. He gave them new ones. The Messiah they followed told them that those who leave behind "houses or brothers or sisters or father or mother or children or lands, for my name's sake, will receive a hundredfold and will inherit eternal life" (Matt. 19:29). Through adoption into Christ, the word *brother* really means something.

Do you notice the loneliness all around us, in metropolitan alleys and roadside barrooms and suburban bedrooms? What does our gospel have to say to the hotel maintenance man who overhears his co-workers laughing that they saw him crying about the fact that his wife left, with their children, this morning? What does our gospel say to the young woman who misses her family back in Illinois but who can't face them since she's become a porn "star" in California? What do we say to the friendless corporate executive as he runs in a caffeine-fueled mania from his bed to his truck to his office and back again every day? What do we say about ourselves when we know the layout of a house on a television drama better than the layout of our next-door neighbor's home?

We're all designed for community—for brothers and sisters. That's why feminists speak so much about how powerful "sister-hood" is. It's why radical terrorist cells refer to their "brothers" who are readying themselves, too, for the revolution. It's why members of fraternities and sororities on college campuses name themselves "brothers" and "sisters." We all will find a brotherhood, for good or for ill, whether it's in a labor union, an international peacekeeping organization, or the Ku Klux Klan. We'll identify ourselves by who is "one of us"—part of our "tribe." Unfortunately, this brotherhood is skin-deep.

Our churches fall for the same thing all the time. We can buy Bibles in niche editions—in the colors of our favorite sports team or with study notes custom-made for our demographic group, whether we're recovering alcoholics or single mothers or theological intellectuals. We order our worship services around our age groups, with music designed to remind each generation of whatever was playing at the youth rallies of their college days. Our congregations are made up of people who look, talk, and think just like we do. And it never occurs to us that this is the same kind of unity the world has to offer. Even in our churches, we seem to identify ourselves more according to the corporate brands we buy and the political parties we support than with each other.

Our adoption means, though, that we find a different kind of unity. In Christ, we find Christ. We don't have our old identities based on race or class or life situation. The Spirit drives us from Babel to Pentecost, which is why "the works of the flesh" Paul warns about include "enmity, strife, jealousy, fits of anger, rivalries, dissensions, divisions, envy" and so forth (Gal. 5:19–21). When we find our identity anywhere other than Christ, our churches will be made up of warring partisans rather than loving siblings. And we'll picture to the world an autopsied Body of Christ, with a little bit of Jesus for everyone, all on our own terms (1 Cor. 1:12–13).

What would it mean, though, if we took the radical notion of being brothers and sisters seriously? What would happen if your church saw an elderly woman no one would ever confuse with "cool" on her knees at the front of the church praying with a body-pierced fifteen-year-old anorexic girl? What would happen if your church saw a white millionaire corporate vice president being mentored by a Latino minimum wage-earning janitor because both know the janitor is more mature in the things of Christ?

Here's where, I think, the nub of the whole issue lies. Adoption would become a priority in our churches if our churches themselves saw our brotherhood and sisterhood in the church itself rather than in our fleshly identities. For some Christians—maybe for you— it's hard to imagine how an African-American could love a white Ukrainian baby, how a Haitian teenager could call Swedish parents "Mom" and "Dad." Of course that's hard to imagine, when so many of our churches can't even get over differences as trivial as musical style.

If we had fewer "white" churches and "black" churches, fewer "blue-collar" churches and "white-collar" churches, maybe we'd see better what Jesus tells us when he says we've come into a new household with one Spirit, one Father, one Christ. In fact, maybe the reason we wonder whether "adopted" children can "really" be brothers and sisters is because we so rarely see it displayed in our pews.

If this will ever happen, though, we have to learn to discover who we really are, together, as the adopted children of God. That isn't easy because our identity is constantly questioned—by our circumstances, by our consciences, by the accusing powers in the air around us.

I remember standing in that courtroom in Russia, giving the judge there the new names of our boys. The court was issuing new birth certificates, with these new Americanized names. The judge stammered out the names we'd given her, with her thick accent: "Benjamin Jacob Moore" and "Timothy Russell Moore." These names were, legally now, who they were. But they didn't know it.

We knew these boys were adjusting to their new identity when they started turning around when we said "Benjamin" or "Timothy." There came a day when one could cry out "Maxim" or "Sergei," and no one would respond. Those old names now meant nothing to them. They seemed to them to be someone else's names, and they were.

Some people would think we've done something wrong by renaming these boys. One book for adoptive parents advises against it because it can "interfere with the continuity of the child's life" or "interfere with their sense of self."[2] We didn't agree. We see naming as part of a welcome—the American names represent the fact that the children are now part of an American family. They're not foreigners, geographically or emotionally. When parents name a child, they're welcoming him; they're identifying him with them, forever.

In our day, names tend to be doled out at the whim of parents' wishes and cultural fads. We name a child what sounds good to us, and what sounds good to us is shaped by what kinds of names seem relatively familiar to us. That's why every third girl in my classes in school was named "Stephanie," and why my sons play with so many girls named "Madison" now. When you hear the names "Harold" or "Rupert," you assume you're dealing with someone in an older generation, and no one expects to find an elderly woman named "Tiffany" these days. In a generation there'll be lots of nursing homes filled with men named "Conner" and women named "Emma." Those names will sound as old as "Milton" or "Gertrude" sounds today. Sometimes a child is named after a family member or a cherished friend, but even then the options are limited by custom. A dear old uncle named "John" is more likely to be honored with a namesake than an uncle named "Ebenezer" (though Ebenezer is a great biblical name, and I hope it comes back).

In the world of the Bible, though, a name said something about who you are, or at least who your parents expected you to become. Esau was named that because he was born red and hairy (Gen. 25:25). Jacob got his name from wrestling with his brother in the birth canal (Gen. 25:26). Both grow into their names, with Esau acting like a beast for red stew (Gen. 25:29–34) and Jacob wrestling with God (Gen. 32:22–32).

A name is important to one's identity. And that's why in the story of our fathers and mothers God keeps changing people's names.

After all, the people of God never considered themselves "sons

---

[2] Holly van Gulden and Lisa M. Bartels-Rabb, *Real Parents, Real Children: Parenting the Adopted Child* (New York: Crossroad, 2007), 96.

of Terah" or even "sons of Abram." They were sons of *Abraham*, a name that means "the father of a multitude of nations" (Gen. 17:5). That name seemed nonsensical at the time for this childless home-less man. It seemed almost a mockery to call his barren old wife a "princess," as the name "Sarah" means (Gen. 17:15). The children of Israel, furthermore, were children of *Israel*. That identity reflects another name change, when the one whose name meant "deceiver," Jacob, wrestled with God on the riverbank. God named him "Israel" because he had struggled with God and men and won (Gen. 32:28). It sure didn't seem as though Israel had won—on the run from his angry brother, limping away from his encounter with God.

But God names the things as though they are and then makes them that way (Rom. 4:17). The same thing has happened with us in our adoption.

Our God tells us he's not ashamed to be named the God of Abraham, Isaac, and Jacob—he's identified himself as such for mil-lennia (Heb. 11:16). More importantly, he's identified himself as the God and Father of Jesus Christ. Let's remember that "Jesus" is a new name. The Word of the Father is not properly called "Jesus" until he is so named. And he is named "Jesus" by a Galilean carpenter, probably without the equivalent of a grade-school education, who believes what he heard from an angel. The name told a story: "He will save his people from their sins" (Matt. 1:21).

Think for a moment about how even in the name of Jesus, God is showing he is not ashamed of you. This name is the one that God promised Abraham he'd uplift. The very glory of God itself resounds through the universe when "at the name of Jesus" every knee is bowed (Phil. 2:9–11). Even the demons, when they shriek out, "Jesus of Nazareth . . . [We] know who you are" (Mark 1:24; cf. Luke 4:34) tremble at the fearful promise of that name—and must recognize that he is his Father's Son. On the great and terrible day of the Lord, Satan himself will be forced, through demonically clenched teeth, to mouth the same word the angel once spoke to Mary, the name each one of us in Christ has cried out to for salvation: Jesus.

In his ancient blessing of his people, God commanded Aaron and his sons to "put my name upon the people of Israel, and I will bless them" (Num. 6:27). Little did they imagine just how he'd do this. He hides his people in One who is named Immanuel—"God with us" (Isa. 7:14), who is named Jesus—"Yahweh saves." As we bear the name of Christ, that's our name now.

Even in the saying of his name—Jesus—we're telling the old, old story of amazing grace. In the saying of that name, our God is telling us that he isn't ashamed of even the least of us, Jesus' brothers.

When Jesus asks his disciples who the Son of Man is speculated to be, various names are rattled off—John, Elijah, Jeremiah, and so forth. When asked for Jesus' identity, one of them announces what God had already voiced: "You are the Christ, the Son of the living God" (Matt. 16:16). Interestingly, Jesus refers to this disciple first by his given name—Simon, the son of John. Jesus, though, gives him a new name—Peter—a rock. Again, the name seems incongruous. The "rock" isn't so solid when Jesus is arrested, and he runs. But Jesus knew what was in store.

The location of his name change is a place called Caesarea Philippi, a region named after the ruler. Caesar's name, it was believed, could be preserved through branding a piece of ground after him. I'll bet it seemed as though that place would last forever. But hidden in the heavenly places is a New Jerusalem, a city that will one day come down and transform the universe. The gates of that city have names—the names, John tells us, of the twelve tribes of Israel (Rev. 21:12). The foundation stones of that city have names too—the names of the twelve apostles of Jesus (Rev. 21:14). Caesar's name is nowhere to be found.

Only in light of Jesus' identity—the Son of the Father—did Peter learn who he was to be. Only there did he find where he fit in the household of God. The same is true for all of us. When we lose our identity, we find it in Christ.

If you're in Christ, he's given you a new name (Rev. 2:17), a name you've never heard and that wouldn't make sense to you right now. It would be like yelling "Timothy Moore" in the halls of an orphanage when he was an infant. But you'll get used to it. Other re-names, like Israel and Abraham and Peter and Paul, didn't make sense either, at first.

More important than your name, however, is hearing it called out by One you've come to know, or rather who has come to know you. When you see him for the first time face-to-face, when your legal adoption is fully realized, the Spirit within you will cry out, "Abba! Father!" And you'll hear another voice, louder than all the others, cry out the same thing. You'll turn to see him, the Messiah of Israel, the Emperor of the universe, Jesus of Nazareth. And you'll call him "brother."

OUR ADOPTED INHERITANCE

When Maria and I at long last received the call that the legal process was over, and we returned to Russia to pick up our new sons, we found that their transition from orphanage to family was more difficult than we had supposed. We dressed the boys in outfits our parents had bought for them. We nodded our thanks to the orphanage personnel and walked out into the sunlight, to the terror of the two boys.

They'd never seen the sun, and they'd never felt the wind. They had never heard the sound of a car door slamming or felt like they were being carried along a road at 100 miles an hour. I noticed that they were shaking and reaching back to the orphanage in the distance. Suddenly it wasn't a stranger asking, "Are they brothers?" They seemed to be asking it, nonverbally but emphatically, about themselves.

I whispered to Sergei, now Timothy, "That place is a pit! If only you knew what's waiting for you—a home with a mommy and a daddy who love you, grandparents and great-grandparents and cousins and playmates and McDonald's Happy Meals!"

But all they knew was the orphanage. It was squalid, but they had no other reference point. It was *home*.

We knew the boys had acclimated to our home, that they trusted us, when they stopped hiding food in their high chairs. They knew there would be another meal coming, and they wouldn't have to fight for the scraps. This was the new normal.

They are now thoroughly Americanized, perhaps too much so, able to recognize the sound of a microwave *ding* from forty yards away. I still remember, though, those little hands reaching for the orphanage. And I see myself there.

The New Testament teaching on the adoption of believers in Christ isn't a reassuring metaphor for the fatherhood of God and the brotherhood of man. Adoption doesn't simply tell us who we are. It is a legal entitlement, one we are prone to forget. "If children, then heirs—heirs of God and fellow heirs with Christ," the Spirit tells us (Rom. 8:17).

I don't know about you, but inheritance was something I, growing up in my working-class world, never imagined would apply to me. An inheritance was something rich people left for their kids—for the spoiled trust-fund heirs who might speed around Malibu in their sports cars. It's hard for us to imagine the place of inheritance in the world in which our Bible was first revealed.

In the world of the Bible, one's identity and one's vocation are all bound up in who one's father is. Men are called "son of" all of their lives (for instance, "the sons of Zebedee" or "Joshua, son of Nun"). There are no guidance counselors in ancient Canaan or first-century Capernaum, helping "teenagers" determine what they want "to be" when they "grow up." A young man watches his father, learns from him, and follows in his vocational steps. This is why "the sons of Zebedee" are right there with their father when Jesus finds them, "in their boat mending the nets" (Mark 1:19–20).

The inheritance was the engine of survival, passed from father to son, an economic pact between generations. To be an orphan was to lose one's inheritance. To lose one's inheritance was to pilfer for survival. To pilfer for survival usually meant winding up somebody's slave, just so you could have enough food to eat.

This inheritance structure is a picture of something deeper, more real—the inheritance that a Father God gives to those who share in his image. The Bible identifies Jesus as the One who inherits the promises made to Abraham, Isaac, and Israel. He is the One of whom it is said, "You are my Son" (Ps. 2:7), to whom the Father promises to make "the nations your heritage, and the ends of the earth your possession" (Ps. 2:8).

This inheritance has to do, again, with the old controversies over circumcision. The Jewish believers in the early church weren't to look to their biological ancestry for their inheritance. They were law-breakers whose only inheritance was death (Rom. 2–3). They were to look instead to the One in whom all the promises of God find their "Yes," the Lord Jesus (2 Cor. 1:20).

You see, that's the whole story of redemption. The universe was meant to be a home—where the image-bearers of God rule and serve under their Father. It was all to be ours. The primeval insurrection in the garden, though, turned the universe into an orphanage—the heirs were gone, done in by their appetites. A serpent now holds the cosmos in captivity, driving along the deposed rulers as his slaves. The whole universe is now an orphanage.

But then there's Jesus.

When we were still orphans, Christ became a substitute orphan for us. Though he was a son, he took on the humiliation of a slave and the horror of death (Phil. 2:6–8). Jesus walked to that far country with us, even to the depths of the hog pen that we'd made our home, and hung on a tree abandoned by his Father in our place.

Only he could do this because only he, the one sinless human, didn't have the cosmic blackmail against him that the Accuser can call up for all of us. The Lord Christ simply announces that "the ruler of this world is coming. He has no claim on me" (John 14:30).

Jesus' attitude is similar to what yours would be if a co-worker challenged you to a lie detector test for being part of an Islamic terrorist cell. You wouldn't cower under your desk (I'm assuming here that you're actually *not* a member of an Islamic terrorist cell) because

you know it isn't true. Jesus doesn't fear Satan's accusation because
he has nothing to hide—from the demonic watchers, from himself, or
from his Father. He is truth, and the truth makes him free indeed.

We cannot consider our adoption as children of God without
turning to the cross. When Jesus is stapled to this Roman torture
device, he bears the full weight of the curse of an orphan creation.
The apostle Paul is able to speak of us as receiving adoption as sons
only because Jesus becomes "a curse for us." In the gospel, the Holy
Spirit simply announces, "for it is written, 'Cursed is everyone who
is hanged on a tree'—so that in Christ Jesus the blessing of Abraham
might come to the Gentiles, so that we might receive the promised
Spirit through faith" (Gal. 3:13–14).

On a Friday two thousand years ago, a Roman soldier strikes a
spear into the dead, bloodied flesh of this Man. Some government
employee pulls spikes from the carcass melded to wood, then goes
home and scrubs off the blood of Christ as he washes up for dinner. He may toss his children in the air with hands still embedded
with the blood of Jesus under his fingernails. The body removal has
to happen before dark; his body can't hang on that tree overnight
because Israel "shall not defile your land that the LORD your God is
giving you for an inheritance" (Deut. 21:23).

But God lifts Jesus out of his hole in the ground and gives him
the universe as his inheritance. The curse is lifted—for Jesus and for
all who are found in him.

The trauma of leaving the orphanage was unexpected to me
because I knew how much better these boys' life would soon be. I
thought they knew too. But they had no idea. They couldn't conceive
of anything other than the status quo. My whispering to my boys,
"You won't miss that orphanage" is only a shadow of something
I should have known already. Our Father tells us that we too are
unable to grasp what's waiting for us—and how glorious it really
is. It's hard for us to long for an inheritance to come, a harmonious
Christ-ruled universe, when we've never seen anything like it.

We just can't imagine "the glory that is to be revealed to us"

(Rom. 8:18). That's why it's so important to have "the eyes of your hearts enlightened, that you may know what is the hope to which he has called you, what are the riches of his glorious inheritance in the saints" (Eph. 1:18).

The Jewish and Gentile congregations in the first century were to find their security in Christ, not in the social and economic hierarchies of the Roman Empire. The churches were to long for the inheritance to come, a cosmos flowing with milk and honey, and not, as their fathers before them, for the slavery from which they came (Deut. 8:14; Rom. 8:15; Gal. 4:7–11).

This inheritance, then, belongs to all of us who, through adoption, are the sons of God. Perhaps you're a little uncomfortable with the way I'm wording this. Maybe you're silently mouthing the words, "and daughters" after all of my references to "sons." Maybe you're wondering if I'm just careless or if I'm so retrograde in my gender views that I'm just forgetting about women and girls altogether. After all, this inheritance belongs to the "sisters" too, not just to the brothers, right?

Some Bible translations translate adoption passages such as Galatians 3:26 to indicate that we are all sons *and daughters* of God through faith in Christ. Sometimes pastors will add as an aside, "and daughters" or "and sisters" to their reading of the adoption passages, to let the women and girls in the congregation know that they're included in this adopting act of their God. I understand what such people are trying to do; I just don't think they're inclusive enough.

Yes, the sonship we have in Jesus applies to both men and women, to both slaves and free, to both Jews and Gentiles (Gal. 3:28). But it's important that we see *why* that's so. We have, as Paul writes, "put on Christ" (Gal. 3:27) and thus share his identity as Abraham's offspring. We are all then "heirs according to promise" (Gal. 3:29). The Galatians—and all of us in Christ—have received adoption as *sons*.

Those reading the apostolic letters for the first time would have understood completely that an inheritance didn't go to the daughter of a tribal patriarch. She received her inheritance through her husband. That's why even we contemporary Westerners retain the act of a father "giving away his daughter" at a wedding ceremony. The inheritance, though, went to the sons, and particularly to the firstborn son.

The apostle Paul knew Greek. He easily could have written to the Galatian or Roman congregations that they are sons and daughters of God. In one very important sense, that's precisely true. We don't lose our sexual differentiation when we are united to Christ, as the apostles make quite clear elsewhere. But in the context of inheritance, Paul could not have written "sons and daughters" without completely losing the meaning of his argument. He speaks of "sons" not because the gospel is anti-woman, but because it is not.

Had the Bible said "sons and daughters," the men in the congregations could have neatly divided the issue of identity from the issue of inheritance. The women, they might have concluded, can pray and relate to God as Father. They're daughters of God. The men, though, would also inherit the promises—the land, the rule, the kingdom. The Jewish believers easily could have hopped around the issue here in much the same way.

The Gentiles, they could have reasoned, are "the daughters of God"—with a relationship to him as Father—but they have no claim to the inheritance; that belongs to the sons, the offspring of Abraham. But the Holy Spirit is breathing out something far more revolutionary than that. If we are hidden in Christ, we are no longer male or female, slave or free, Jew or Gentile; our inheritance is whatever belongs to him.

But our inheritance, like our identity, is hard to believe.

We must learn to be children, not orphans. When my sons arrived in the family, their legal status was not ambiguous at all. They were our kids. But their wants and affections were still atrophied by a year in the orphanage. They didn't know that flies on their faces were bad. They didn't know that a strange man feeding them their first scary gulps of solid food wasn't a torturer. Life in the cribs alone must have seemed to them like freedom. That's what I was missing about the biblical doctrine of adoption. Sure, it's glorious in the long run. But it sure seems like hell in the short run.

My whispering to my boys, "You won't miss that orphanage" is only a shadow of something I should have known. God pronounces Israel his "son," brings the Israelites through the baptismal waters of judgment, and promises to give them an inheritance, and they long for the fleshpots of Egypt (Ex. 16:1–3). They'd rather be slaves than sons, because at least they could trust the slave driver to give them what they needed.

The pull toward slave nostalgia is a real danger for all of us. Satan once held all of us in "lifelong slavery" through our "fear of death" (Heb. 2:15). The temptation for all of us is to shrink back to the petty protectors we once hid behind, to be slaves again to placate the Grim Reaper. That's why Paul could thunder to the Galatians, "Formerly, when you did not know God, you were enslaved to those that by nature are not gods. But now that you have come to know God, or rather to be known by God, how can you turn back again to the weak and worthless elementary principles of the world, whose slaves you want to be once more?" (Gal. 4:8–9). Perhaps the most striking aspect of this rebuke is the apostle's insistence that the believers *want* to be slaves again. Why? They're afraid.

Jesus, by contrast, is pronounced the "beloved Son" of God, is likewise brought through the waters of baptism, and is then tempted by the Evil One to believe that a Father who promises him bread would give him only stones (Matt. 3:13–4:4). Listening to his Father's voice, even to the point of crucifixion and apparent abandonment by God, he "learned obedience through what he suffered," and "he was heard" (Heb. 5:7–8). Jesus isn't fearful because he knows who he is.

Our adoption, remember, conforms us to Christ's image. So we'll walk this path to maturity too, the path Jesus walked before us. "For you did not receive the spirit of slavery to fall back into fear," Paul tells the church at Rome, "but you have received the spirit of adoption as sons" (Rom. 8:15). That has to be said. It's not obvious. It's hard to believe there's a kingdom waiting for us.

We don't fully believe that our new Father will feed us, so we hang on to our scraps and long for the regimented schedules of the orphanage from which we've come. And when our Father pushes us along to new tastes, we pout that he's not good to us. But he's readying us for glory, preparing us to take our place on thrones as heirs.

Part of this path to maturity is in the past, in the history of God's intervention of redemption. It's absurd to try to live under the shadows of the Law of Moses, Paul tells the church at Galatia. The Law, he says, once held us in captivity (Gal. 3:23), but it's a very different kind of captivity than that of Pharaoh or Satan. The Law, Paul says, was "our guardian until Christ came, in order that we might be justified by faith" (Gal. 3:24). We are indeed heirs, he writes, but "the heir, so long as he is a child, is no different from a slave, though he is the owner of everything, but he is under guardians and managers until the date set by his father" (Gal. 4:1–2).

What he's saying is that until a child reaches maturity, he resembles in some ways an employee. He lives in his own house—he may even inherit it all one day—but he still has to be put in a playpen to keep him from barreling down the stairs. He still has to have his food chosen for him. He still has to have rules put in place to keep him from throwing electronic appliances into the bathtub or refrigerating the puppies. There was a time when I had to tell my sons, repeatedly, "We're the kind of people who don't belch in front of ladies." I don't expect to have to say those words at their respective wedding ceremonies.

The Law of Moses marks out the people of God, for a time, in some specific ways—telling them what to eat and what to wear, giving them a specific earthly locale at which to worship with specific signs pointing to the kind of God they served. That Law, though, didn't bring about the inheritance; it pointed to the promise (Gal. 3:18). It penned in the people of God, making them distinct from the other nations and showing them God's perspective on their own sin, "until the offspring should come to whom the promise had been made" (Gal. 3:19). The Law was waiting for Jesus.

When the Christ-followers in the first century, however, are deceived into going backward—to circumcision, food regulations, and so forth—they are infantilizing themselves and repudiating Christ. They'd rather cling to the household employee Moses than to the household heir he served, Jesus (Heb. 3:1–6). They are, then, like the child who cries for the day-care worker when his mother comes to pick him up or who starts to call the part-time babysitter "Mama." It's a tragedy.

Part of this push to maturity is going on right now in your life, and in mine. If we belong to our Father, he disciplines us—as sons, not as illegitimate children. Our Father warns us not to sell our inheritance for a mess of pottage, as our great-great-great-great-great-great-uncle did a long time ago (Heb. 12:3–17). Why would we covet what seems important to Wall Street or Hollywood or Madison Avenue when we have waiting for us mountain ranges and waterfalls and distant galaxies to rule with Christ as the resurrected sons of the new creation?

That's why the unity of the church is not simply in a common liberation but also in a common frustration. The Spirit drives us to discontentedness with the status quo, and so we call out together for our Father's attention.

The *Abba* cry just might be the most easily misunderstood and misinterpreted aspect of the biblical revelation of our adoption. How many of us have heard *Abba* described as an infant cooing out the words "Da-da" or "Papa"? This cry though, in the context of the Scriptures, is not an infantile cooing. The *Abba* cry is a scream. It's less the sound of a baby giggling up into his father's face, and more the sound of a child screaming "Daddy!" as his face is being ripped apart by a rabid bulldog. It is primal scream theology.

The Bible tells us, "In the days of his flesh, Jesus offered up prayers and supplications, with loud cries and tears, to him who was able to save him from death, and he was heard because of his reverence" (Heb. 5:7). Jesus in the Garden of Gethsemane isn't placidly staring, straight-backed with hands against a rock, into the sky as a shaft of light beams down on his face, as in so many of our paintings and church stained-glass window artistry. He is screaming to his Father for deliverance, to the point that the veins in his temples burst into drops of blood (Luke 22:39–44). That's the *Abba* cry. It's the scream of the crucified.

Of all the disturbing aspects of the orphanage in which we found our boys, one stands out above all the others in its horror. It was quiet. The place was filled with an eerie silence, quieter than the Library of Congress, despite the fact that there were cribs full of babies in every room. If you listened intently enough, you could hear the sound of gentle rocking—as babies rocked themselves back and forth in their beds. They didn't cry because no one responded to their cries. So they stopped. That's dehumanizing in its horror.

The first moment I knew the boys received us, in some strange and preliminary way, was the moment we walked out of the room for the last time on that first trip. When little Maxim, now Benjamin, fell back in his crib and cried—the first time I ever heard him do it—it was because, for whatever reason, he seemed to think he'd be heard and, for whatever reason, he no longer liked the prospect of being alone in the dark.

That's where the Spirit is leading us, in Christ. The Holy Spirit doesn't lead us to be the toothy, giddy caricature of a "Spirit-filled" Christian. The Spirit leads us to see when we are in enemy-occupied territory, and he teaches us to rage against that machine. We're frustrated right now when we see images of a python swallowing a pig on a nature program on television, when we see a billboard for a divorce attorney, when we hear of children swept away by a mudslide in the Third World, when we find ourselves gossiping about an acquaintance. The Spirit leads us to cry out with the rest of the universe, "O God, deliver us from this! This is not how it's supposed to be!"

It is through this kind of praying that we know we have "received the Spirit of adoption as sons" (Rom. 8:15). Through this, "The Spirit himself bears witness with our spirit that we are children of God, and if children, then heirs" (Rom. 8:16–17). Sometimes this passage confuses believers because we assume this means there's an internal prompt, reassuring us that we're really children of God. We assume this means a kind of peace in our heart, a tranquillity of assurance. It's actually the opposite.

The *Abba* cry is a groan. Paul tells the church at Rome that because of the curse, "the whole creation has been groaning together in the pains of childbirth until now" (Rom. 8:22). It's hard for us to hear the tenor of the terror in that verse, living with the kind of medical technology we have all around us. We think of "the pains of childbirth" as unpleasantness—something that, if a woman so chooses, can be lessened with anesthetic. Even a woman who decides to bear a baby through "natural childbirth" almost never in our context does so naturally. There's always a kind of medical assistance, even if it's just the knowledge that an ambulance can be called if a home birth goes badly.

For our foremothers, though, and even now for many of our sisters around the world, the pangs of childbearing meant, and mean, a sense of life or death desperation. One doesn't know whether the pain means things are going well or if one is going to die. The whole universe, Paul says, is screaming out like that—"longing for the revealing of the sons of God" (Rom. 8:19). Yes, the creation "waits" patiently, but it's a patience that screams along the way.

But it's not just the creation screaming. Paul writes that "we ourselves, who have the firstfruits of the Spirit, groan inwardly as we wait eagerly for adoption as sons, the redemption of our bodies" (Rom. 8:23). As we pray, Paul says, "the Spirit himself intercedes for us with groanings too deep for words" (Rom. 8:26).

When we recognize the groaning of the universe—and groan with it—we are confessing our own complicity in the curse. The anguish of pain in childbirth in the prophets, after all, is related sometimes to the reaction of the rulers of this world to the revelation of Mount Zion (Ps. 48:6). It's the realization of a kingdom that's crumbling into the sand beneath it. We're not able to rule over this chaos, and so we breathe out, "Lord, have mercy on me, a sinner." We recognize then, all around us, the need for a crucified Christ, and we endure suffering because we know that it is only in his shed blood and pierced flesh that the universe will be restored.

Once at a gathering with several friends, I stopped listening to the person talking to me and crooked my head to overhear a conversation that another (much older and wiser) man was having with others. He was speaking of ancient Jewish patterns of prayer and how different they are from contemporary patterns. Our Jewish and early Christian forefathers, he said, would rarely have prayed silently with heads bowed. Instead, they prayed noisily, with their arms outstretched to the heavens. We know this from the Old Testament Scriptures as well as from early Christian catacomb art.

I knew this, but what made the hair stand up on my arms was the older man's characterization of the physicality of this stance. He stood with his arms stretched upward and asked, "Does this not look like a toddler, in virtually every human culture, crying out to his parents for food or attention?" He continued, "And is it not also cruciform? How is it our Lord Jesus would have cried out, 'My God, my God, why hast thou forsaken me'? Was it not with arms stretched out to the heavens, as a child to his father?"[3]

This is why suffering is so important. It isn't self-flagellation, as though someone in a monastery in the Sahara is necessarily any holier than someone who's not. All believers in Christ, the Scripture teaches, will suffer—all of us. You will be glorified, Paul says, *if* you suffer with him. The problem with too many of us is not that we don't suffer, but that we assume that only Third World Christians or heroic missionaries are suffering. My boys didn't know that they were suffering in Russia; they would feel it as suffering now.

---

[3] I am indebted to Patrick Henry Reardon, pastor of All Saints Antiochian Orthodox Church in Chicago, for this observation.

The Bible speaks, paradoxically, of our adoption in Christ as a past event but also as a future one. "We wait eagerly for adoption as sons," Paul writes, and he tells us what that looks like: "the redemption of our bodies" (Rom. 8:23). We legally belong to our Father. But as long as our bodies are dying, as long as the universe is heaving in pain around us, it sure looks like we're orphans still. We know that we're children by faith, not yet by sight.

But we get too comfortable with this orphanage universe. We sit in our pews, or behind our pulpits, knowing that our children watch "Christian" cartoons instead of slash films. We vote for the right candidates and know all the right "worldview" talking points. And we're content with the world we know, just adjusted a little for our identity as Christians. That's precisely why so many of us are so atrophied in our prayers, why our prayers rarely reach the level of "groanings too deep for words" (Rom. 8:26). We are too numbed to be as frustrated as the Spirit is with the way things are.

"I know you think this terrestrial orphanage is home," our Father tells us through prophets and apostles and consciences and imaginations, "but it's a pit compared to home." Or as the Spirit says through the apostle Paul's adoption teaching, "For I consider that the sufferings of this present time are not worth comparing with the glory that is to be revealed to us" (Rom. 8:18).

I want to see that orphanage one more time. When the boys are a little older, maybe twelve or fourteen, I plan to make the trip again, with them. I want them to see, to feel, where they came from. It's hard to imagine now what they'll think of it. They'll probably hate Russian food as much as I do and will look forward to slipping off with me to the McDonald's in Moscow when we can find it.

At the orphanage I'm sure their eyes will widen as we walk up those creaking steps into that horror movie-looking front door. They'll probably go limp inside, just like I did, when they see all those abandoned toddlers peering out from the corners of the doors inside. Maybe they'll try to replay in their minds the circumstances of the nights they were born. I'm not sure what all they'll think of the orphanage. But I'm quite sure they won't call it home.

I do want to see the orphanage again. More importantly, I want to leave it again. Maybe Benjamin and Timothy and I will take a picture together in front of it before we leave, to hang on our wall at home. I want to look in the backseat and see no hands reaching backward. I want to see two young men, maybe with sunglasses on, looking forward, smiling into the sunshine ahead of them. I can only pray that I'll do the same as I see my own orphanage in the rearview mirror.

CONCLUSION

Recently my sons and I were in a bookstore near our home, buying a Mother's Day card for their mother (yes, their *real* mother I would add). As we were checking out at the cash register, the sales clerk said, "Wow. Are all four of these boys yours? How old are they?" I pointed to them in sequence and said, "Six, six, two and a half, and one year." As soon as I finished, Benjamin added his own comment, "And don't ask if we're brothers 'cause it drives him crazy."

That's an exaggeration, I think. It doesn't drive me crazy—anymore. As a matter of fact, it doesn't much bother me anymore. I hope that's because I'm more spiritually mature and less easily offended. It may be because Timothy is so much taller than Benjamin now that people assume he's much older than his brother so we don't get the "are they twins?" question. Or maybe it's because our family is so secure now that I don't feel threatened by the question. But it is helpful to me to remember sometimes how hollow I felt when I first answered those questions about "real" brothers and "real" parents, about their place in our family. And I remind myself that I've been just as far from "getting it" as the good-natured questioners I have resented.

The real struggle for me shouldn't be the occasional rude question about my sons' identity; it should be the ongoing question about my own. Maybe such questions bothered me so much because they are being asked about me, all the time, within the echo chamber of my own fallen psyche and by unseen rebel angels all around. Are you really a son of the living God? Does your God really know you? Does this biblical story really belong to you? Are these really your brothers and sisters? Do you really belong here? The question of identity related to adoption was so desperate because it challenged the authenticity of my family. But more than that, it challenged the authenticity of the gospel I'd believed since childhood.

The warfare that crackles all around us is quite like that. The powers threatened by the inheritance of which we will speak next want to redirect our minds from who we are in Christ; they want to point us instead to our own flesh—to our impending death, to our instinctual resemblance to Satan. The problem is, we are so easily outwitted by such designs. We veer from a fleshly self-sufficiency to a fleshly despair to a fleshly tribalism. And in all of this we lose sight of Christ. In adoption we find ourselves—in Jesus. We see something that we cannot perceive with our eyes.

Our adoption is about more than just belonging. Our adoption is about the day when the graves of this planet will be emptied, when the great assembly of Christ's church will be gathered before the Judgment Seat. On that day, the accusing principalities and powers will probably look once more at us—former murderers and fornicators and idolaters, formerly uncircumcised in flesh or in heart—and they may ask one more time, "So are they brothers?" The hope of adopted children like my sons—and like me—is that the voice that once thundered over the Jordan will respond, one last time, "They are now."

3

Joseph of Nazareth vs.
Planned Parenthood

What's at Stake When We Talk about Adoption

I PLAYED A COW in my first-grade Christmas pageant, and I had more lines than the kid who played Joseph. He was a prop, or so it seemed, for Mary, the plastic doll in the manger, and the rest of us. We were just following the script. There's rarely much room in the inn of the contemporary Christian imagination for Joseph, especially among conservative Protestants like me. His only role, it seems, is an usher—to get Mary to the stable in Bethlehem in the first place and then to get her back to the Temple in Jerusalem in order to find the wandering twelve-year-old Jesus.

But there's much more to the Joseph figure.

Joseph serves as a model to follow as we see what's at stake in the issue of adoption. Joseph, after all, is an adoptive father. In some ways, his situation is, of course, far different from that of any reader holding this book right now. In other ways, though, Joseph's mission belongs to all of us. As Joseph images the Father of the fatherless, he shows us how adoption is more than charity. It's spiritual warfare.

ADOPTION AND SPIRITUAL WARFARE

The couple looked familiar to me as I saw them approaching, smiling, pushing a stroller toward me, but I couldn't place their names. It was the annual summer meeting of my denomination, so I was used to renewing old acquaintances from all over the country. The husband was the first to speak, and he told me that he and his wife had met with me about adoption a few years earlier when they were students at the seminary I serve. They wanted me to see the little boy they had adopted, from a former Soviet state. I knelt down to talk with the little fellow as he shyly curled back in his seat. The little boy had beautiful olive skin coloring, looked as though he had Arabic or perhaps Persian roots, and had cute little chubby cheeks. As I played peek-a-boo with the little boy, I asked the parents if they'd had any trouble with bureaucracy along the way.

"The only problem we had was with the judge," the wife said. "The judge thought there was some mistake that we'd want this child because he's dark-skinned. The judge said no one would want a child like that and that there were plenty of light-skinned babies available. He just couldn't believe that we would want him and almost treated us as though we were up to something shady because we did."

I wasn't expecting that, and as I stroked this little boy's cheek, those words struck me: "No one would ever want a child like that." I picked him up from his stroller and hugged him, hoping I wouldn't start crying in front of my denominational peers walking up and down the corridor of the convention hall. "You're loved and wanted," I told him. "Isn't that great?"

After I finished the conversation with the family and went back to the relative inanity of voting on resolutions and motions on the convention floor, I couldn't get the horror of that situation off my mind. How could a judge sit in his chair and deem that lovable child to be unworthy of love simply because of the shade of his skin? What kind of backward Philistines were they dealing with in that courtroom?

And then I remembered that my denomination, in whose delib-erations I then sat, was formed in a dispute with other American Christians over the slavery of other human beings because of the color of their skin. And my people had been on the slaveholders' side. Previous generations of preachers just like me (indeed probably some related to me) had argued that some children were unworthy of freedom because of the shade of their skin. My own ancestors had seen to it that children of a darker skin than themselves were made orphans. As the resolutions flew around the convention hall about "the sanctity of marriage," I realized that previous generations of preachers in this very same context had propped up a system in which parents couldn't marry legally because that would make it more difficult to sell them individually when necessary.

A similar story could be told a billion times over in virtually every human society throughout history. There seems to be an orphan-making urge among us, whether we see it in the slave culture of centuries past or the divorce culture of today. But where does it come from?

In the stories preserved for us by Jesus' disciples Matthew and Luke, we see that Joseph of Nazareth discovers something of the root behind it all. Joseph, after all, finds himself a player in a story that has played out before.

The Gospel of Matthew tells us that King Herod learns from some traveling stargazers that the foreseen birth of the royal son of David is here. Herod is "troubled, and all Jerusalem with him" (Matt. 2:3). Herod pores over the ancient scrolls, not in order to submit to them in faith, but to see how to circumvent this new king. Herod is right, of course. The promised Anointed One is a threat to Herod's tyranny. The son of David will receive, God has promised, a galactic empire, with all his enemies under his feet. Herod protects his position through infanticide. He orders all the male children under two in the region of Bethlehem, the prophesied location of the Davidic king's birth, to be executed by royal decree.

Herod surely didn't think about the fact that he was playing the role of Pharaoh, but he was. This scenario is precisely what had played out thousands of years before when another ruler had his power threatened by the offspring of Abraham.

In the writings of Moses, we see that the Egyptian king saw the people of Israel among his population, that they "were fruitful and increased greatly; they multiplied and grew exceedingly strong, so that the land was filled with them" (Ex. 1:7).

Notice that this description of the Israelites is precisely what God has defined already as blessing. God promises at the creation that he will bless the man and the woman by making them fruitful, multiplying them across the face of the earth (Gen. 1:28). God blesses Abraham by promising to make him fruitful and to multiply his offspring to be as many as the stars of the sky (Gen. 15:5; 17:6).

What God pronounces as blessing, Pharaoh sees as a curse. Why? Pharaoh is worshipping the self as god, and the multiplication of the Hebrew people is a threat to the power of this god. So he seeks to remove that threat by any means necessary. First, he tries oppression, then the murder of infants.

Years later, Herod is another Pharaoh. The blessing of all blessings—the coming of the Christ—is seen by Herod in starkly personal terms. If there was an occupant on David's throne, it meant Herod wouldn't be "King of the Jews" anymore, and that just couldn't be, so he lashed out in murderous rage.

What's noteworthy about both Pharaoh and Herod is that both of them represent nations raging against God's Christ (Ps. 2:1–2). In Pharaoh's case, his rage is against the mass of Abraham's descendants, but this is a multitude that God pronounces as his "firstborn son" (Ex. 4:22–23). God knows that it was from this people, in the fullness of time, from whom he will bring forth his Christ. If Pharaoh exterminates this people group, the consequences would be even greater than genocide; the consequences would be hell for the entire world. Herod knew full well what the old prophecies said about the Messiah. He probably prayed ornate prayers that God would send his promised king in the last days. But when the last days were suddenly upon him, Herod hates Jesus, even just by reputation.

What's also noteworthy about both of these dictators is that both of them take the rage they had against Jesus in particular and directs it toward babies in general. When it's Jesus versus the self, babies are caught in the crossfire. And it's always that way.

Several years ago a friend sent me a copy of what just might be the most chilling Christmas card ever sent through the U.S. mail. The

Planned Parenthood Federation of America, the nation's leading provider of abortions, unveiled a holiday greeting card in support of the group's commitment to "reproductive freedom." The card was beautifully designed, complete with embossed snowflakes and stars made of glitter. Across the card was the caption "Choice on Earth."

Across the country, evangelicals and Roman Catholics and others were outraged. In terms of in-your-face religious hostility, that card can only be compared to a Hanukkah card featuring a menorah twisted into a swastika. How could an organization devoted to something that orthodox Christians of every tradition in every generation have abhorred turn a phrase from the Christian Scripture into a fund-raising event for their cause?

It turns out, though, that the Planned Parenthood greeting card is quite appropriate for the time of year when Christians celebrate the Incarnation. We ought to be reminded that Jesus is not born into a gauzy, snowy winter wonderland of sweetly-singing angels and cute reindeer nuzzling one another at the side of his manger. He is born into a war zone. And at the very rumor of his coming, Herod—the Planned Parenthood of his day—vows to see him dead, right along with thousands of his brothers.

Again, it's always that way. The Bible tells us so. Whether through political machinations such as those of Pharaoh and Herod, through military conquests in which bloodthirsty armies rip babies from pregnant mothers' wombs (Amos 1:13), or through the more "routine" seeming family disintegration and family chaos, children are always hurt. Human history is riddled with their corpses.

Why? It's because there are not just impersonal economic and sociological factors at work. "The course of this world" is driven along by "the prince of the power of the air" (Eph. 2:2). Jesus showed his disciple John what the story behind the story is. It's the picture of a woman giving birth to "a male child, one who is to rule all the nations with a rod of iron" (Rev. 12:5). Crouching before this woman's birth canal is a dragon, the Serpent of old, who seeks to "devour" the baby (Rev. 12:4). That dragon then "became furious with the woman and went off to make war on the rest of her offspring" (Rev. 12:17) and has done so ever since.

The demonic powers hate babies because they hate Jesus. When they destroy "the least of these" (Matt. 25:40, 45), the most vulnerable among us, they're destroying a picture of Jesus himself, of the child delivered by the woman who crushes their head (Gen. 3:15). They know the human race is saved—and they're vanquished—by a woman giving birth (Gal. 4:4; 1 Tim. 2:15). They are grinding apart Jesus' brothers and sisters (Matt. 25:40). They are also destroying the very picture of newness of life and of dependent trust that characterizes life in the kingdom of Christ (Matt. 18:4). Children also mean blessing—a perfect target for those who seek only to kill and destroy (John 10:10).

The demonic powers are, we must remember, rebel angels—angels created to be "ministering spirits sent out to serve for the sake of those who are to inherit salvation" (Heb. 1:14). In rebelling against this calling, the servants are in revolt against the sons, and that kind of insurrection leads to murder, as we've seen in other contexts (e.g., Mark 12:1–12). As James tells us, our lust for things we can't have leads to wars among us (James 4:2). The same is true in the heavenly places. The satanic powers want the kingdoms of the universe—and a baby uproots their reign. So they rage all the more against the babies and children who image him. As the wisdom of God announces, "All who hate me love death" (Prov. 8:36).

Satan always uses human passions to bring about his purposes. When new life stands in the way of power—whether that power is a Pharaoh's military stability or a community leader's reputation in light of his teenage daughter's pregnancy—the blood of children often flows. Herod loved his power; so he raged against babies. In the middle of all of this stood Joseph, an unlikely demon-wrestler.

It's easy to shake our heads in disgust at Pharaoh or Herod or Planned Parenthood. It's not as easy to see the ways in which we ourselves often have a Pharaoh-like view of children rather than a

Christlike view.[1] What God calls blessing, we often grumble at as a curse—and for the same reason those old kings did, because they disrupt our life plans. Our "kingdom" may be smaller than that of those old kings, our pyramids and monuments less enduring; but it's all still there. I'm not arguing that parents should have as many children as biologically possible. I'm not arguing that every family is called to adopt children.

I am suggesting, though, that we look at some of the ways in which we refuse to see blessing in something as noisy and frustrating as children. Just last night I huffed around my house, sullen with anger. My son Timothy had accidentally spilled milk on a notebook full of notes for this chapter. He apologized, and I accepted his apology, but I had that look in my eyes and that angry setting to my mouth. It wasn't until this morning that the Spirit convicted me of harboring anger toward a little child, all because he innocently disrupted my plans—my plans to, of all things, write a book about the glory of adoption. What a hypocrite. Children disrupt plans, and blessedly so. They might disrupt yours. It's easy to resent this disruption and lash out against it, perhaps not in murder but in the anger that's the root of murder (Matt. 5:21–22).

It might be that you're reading this book because your spouse wants to adopt, and you're arguing you can't afford it. Maybe you're right. But could it be the Lord is calling you to adopt, and you know you can't "afford" it while maintaining the stuff you have right now? It might be you're reading this book because your son or daughter wants to adopt, and you're thinking about talking them out of it. It's just so expensive, or it's just not the right time. Maybe you're right. But maybe you're just not seeing what's at stake here.

The protection of children isn't charity. It isn't part of a political program fitting somewhere between tax cuts and gun rights or between carbon emission caps and a national service corps. It's spiritual warfare.

---

[1] I am indebted to my friend David Prince for this observation, which he preached to his congregation at Ashland Avenue Baptist Church in Lexington, Kentucky.

Our God forbids Israel from offering their children to Molech, a demon-god who demands the violent sacrifice of human babies (Lev. 20:1–8). Indeed, he denounces Molech by name. He further warns that he will cut off from the people of God not only the one who practiced such sacrifice but also all who "at all close their eyes to that man when he gives one of his children to Molech" (Lev. 20:4). Behind Molech, God recognizes, there is one who is "a murderer from the beginning" (John 8:44).

The spirit of Molech is at work among us even now. Even as you read this page, there are bones of babies being ground to unrecognizable bits, perhaps even a few short miles from where you're sitting. There are babies lying in garbage receptacles, waiting to be taken away as "medical waste." These infants won't have names until Jesus calls them out for the first time. There are little girls waiting in Asia for a knock at the door, for an American businessman who's paid a pimp to be able to sexually assault them. There are children staring out the window of a social worker's office, rubbing their bruises as they hear their mother tell the police why she'll never do it again.

Aborted babies can't say, "*Abba*." But the Father hears their cries anyway. Do we?

The universe is at war, and some babies and children are on the line. The old serpent is coiled right now, his tongue flicking, watching for infants and children he can consume. One night two thousand years ago, all that stood in his way was one reluctant day laborer who decided to be a father.

ADOPTION AND THE IMAGE OF GOD

When we talk about Joseph at all, we spend most of our time talking about what he was *not*. We believe (rightly) with the apostles that Jesus was conceived in a virgin's womb. Joseph was not Jesus' biological father; not a trace of Joseph's sperm was involved in the formation of the embryo Christ. No amount of Joseph's DNA could be found in the dried blood of Jesus peeled from the wood of Golgotha's cross. Jesus was conceived by the Holy Spirit completely apart from the will or exertion of any man.

That noted, though, we need to be careful that we don't reduce Joseph simply to a truthful first-century Bill Clinton: "He did not have sexual relations with that woman." There's much more to be said. Joseph is not Jesus' biological father, but he is his *real* father. In his adoption of Jesus, Joseph is rightly identified by the Spirit speaking through the Scriptures as Jesus' father (Luke 2:41, 48).

Jesus would have said, "*Abba*" first to Joseph.

Jesus' obedience to his father and mother, obedience essential to his law-keeping on our behalf, is directed toward Joseph (Luke 2:51). Jesus does not share Joseph's bloodline, but he claims him as his father, obeying Joseph perfectly and even following in his vocation. When Jesus is tempted in the wilderness, he cites the words of Deuteronomy to counter "the flaming darts of the evil one" (Eph. 6:16). Think about it for a moment—Jesus almost certainly learned those Hebrew Scriptures from Joseph as he listened to him at the woodworking table or stood beside him in the synagogue.

And, perhaps most significantly, if Joseph is *not* "really" the father of Jesus, you and I are going to hell.

Jesus' identity as the Christ, after all, is tied to his identity as the descendant of David, the legitimate heir to David's throne. Jesus saves us as David's son, the offspring of Abraham, the Christ. That human identity came to Jesus through adoption. Matthew and Luke trace Jesus' roots in Abraham and David through the line of Joseph. As the Presbyterian scholar J. Gresham Machen put it, Joseph's adoption of Jesus means Jesus belongs "to the house of David just as truly as if he were in a physical sense the son of Joseph. He was a gift of God to the Davidic house, not less truly, but on the contrary in a more wonderful way than if he had been descended from David by ordinary generation."[2] It is through Joseph that Jesus finds his identity as the fulfillment of the Old Testament promise. It is through Joseph's legal fatherhood of Jesus that "the hopes and fears of all the years"

[2] J. Gresham Machen, *The Virgin Birth of Christ* (New York: Harper, 1930), 129.

find their realization in the final son of Abraham, son of David, and son of Israel.

Joseph's fatherhood is significant for us precisely because of the way the gospel anchors it to the fatherhood of God himself.

Joseph marries the virgin girl, taking the responsibility for the baby on himself. Moreover, he protects the woman and her child by rescuing them from Herod's sword, exiling them in Egypt until the dictator's rampage was ended by death. Interestingly, Matthew tells us, "This was to fulfill what the Lord had spoken by the prophet, 'Out of Egypt I called my son'" (Matt. 2:15). Now, at first glance this seems to be an embarrassing error on the part of the apostle. After all, the Scripture passage he references—from Hosea 11:1—isn't about something in the future but about something in the past. "When Israel was a child, I loved him, and out of Egypt I called my son," God declares in the past tense, speaking of the exodus of the Israelites from Egypt. Isn't Matthew misinterpreting the plain reading of the Bible? No.

Israel, remember, is being called out to bring forth the blessing to the nations, the Christ of God. Israel is the "son" of God precisely because of her relationship to the Christ who is to come. God in the exodus is preparing his people for a final exodus to come in Christ. Jesus sums up in his life the history of Israel and the history of the world, living out this history in obedient trust of his Father. He then fulfills the flight out of Egypt in the same way he fulfills the march into the Promised Land: the promises find their yes and their amen in him, the shadows find their substance in him. It's not that Jesus is the copy of Israel coming out of Egypt, but that Israel coming out of Egypt was the copy—in advance—of Jesus.[3]

Israel wound up in Egypt the first time through violence. The brothers of Israel sought to kill a young dreamer named Joseph. God, though, meant it for good, using the sojourn in Egypt to protect the nation from famine (Gen. 50:20). The Joseph of old told his broth-

---

[3]For a helpful discussion of how Jesus fulfills the "out of Egypt" prophecy, see John Murray, "The Unity of the Old and New Testaments," in *Collected Works*, Vol. 1, *The Claims of Truth* (Edinburgh: Banner of Truth, 1976), 25–26.

ers, "I will provide for you and your little ones" (Gen. 50:21). Joseph of Nazareth pictures his namesake in providing for and protecting Jesus in Egypt. But he also pictures God, the One who brought the people in and out of Egypt, who shields them from the dictator's murderous conspiracies.

Joseph is unique in one sense. He is called to provide for and protect the Christ of God. But in other ways Joseph is not unique at all. All of us, as followers of Christ, are called to protect children. And protecting children doesn't simply mean saving their lives—although it certainly means that—or providing for their material needs—although, again, it does mean that. Governments are called to protect the innocent and to punish evildoers (Rom. 13:1–5), which is why we should work to outlaw abortion, infanticide, child abuse, and other threats to children. Governments and private agencies can play a role in providing economic relief to the impoverished, which is why Christians weigh in on issues such as divorce policy, labor laws, and welfare reform.

But picturing the fatherhood of God means more than these things. His fatherhood is personal, familial. Protecting children means rolling back the curse of fatherlessness, inasmuch as it lies within our power to do so.

When parents care for a child, their child, they're picturing something bigger than themselves. They are an icon of a cosmic reality—the reality of the Father "from whom every family in heaven and on earth is named" (Eph. 3:15).

Joseph's rescue of Jesus isn't the first time the adoption of a child is tied to the exodus event. David sings about God as "Father of the fatherless and protector of widows" who "settles the solitary in a home," tying this reality to God marching before his people through the wilderness toward Canaan (Ps. 68:5–6). God shows this is the kind of God he is. He's the kind of God, the prophet Hosea tells us, of whom we cry out, "In you the orphan finds mercy" (Hos. 14:3).

God everywhere tells us he is seeking to reclaim the marred image of himself in humanity by conforming us to the image of Christ who is the image of the invisible God. As we become Christlike, we become godly. As we become godly, we grow in holiness— differentness from the age around us. This God-imaging holiness means, therefore, an imaging of God's affections, including his love for orphans. After delivering Israel from Egypt and speaking to them from the mountain of Sinai, God tells his people to be like him. "He executes justice for the fatherless and the widow, and loves the sojourner, giving him food and clothing," God says through Moses. "Love the sojourner, therefore, for you were sojourners in the land of Egypt" (Deut. 10:18–19).

Sometimes you might hear some criticize the Bible as "patriarchal." If by this they mean the Bible is about propping up male privilege or self-interest, they're wrong. If they mean the Bible sanctions the abuse of women or denies the dignity and equality of women, they're wrong. But depending on how one defines patriarchy, they're correct that the Bible's patriarchal. The ancient world's concept of patriarchy, after all, wasn't so much about who was "in charge," in the way we tend to think of it, although the father of a family was clearly the head of that family. In the biblical picture, though, the father is responsible to bear the burden for providing for and protecting his family.

When God creates the first human beings, he commands them to "be fruitful and multiply" (Gen. 1:28) and builds into them unique characteristics to carry out this task. The Creator designs the woman to bring forth and nurture offspring. Her name, Eve, means, the Scriptures tell us, "the mother of all living" (Gen. 3:20). The cosmic curse that comes upon the creation shows up, for the woman, in the pain through which she carries out this calling—birth pangs (Gen. 3:16). The man, as the first human father, is to "work the ground from which he was taken" (Gen. 3:23). Adam, made of earth, is to bring forth bread from the earth, a calling that is also frustrated by the curse (Gen. 3:17–19). In this, Adam images a Father who protects and provides for his children.

Thus, Jesus teaches us to pray to a Father who grants us "daily bread" (Matt. 6:11). He points to the natural inclination of a father to give to his son a piece of bread or a fish as an icon of the patriarchy of God: "If you then, who are evil, know how to give good gifts to your children, how much more will your Father who is in heaven give good things to those who ask him" (Matt. 7:11).

Indeed, the apostle Paul charges any father who refuses to provide for his family with being "worse than an unbeliever" (1 Tim. 5:8). In fact, Paul says that such a man has already "denied the faith." Why? It is precisely because being in Christ means recognition of the fatherhood of God. The abandoning or neglectful father blasphemes against such divine fatherhood with a counter-portrayal that is not true to the blessed reality.

Parenting means sacrifice. It seems that every couple of years someone comes out with a psychological or sociological study showing that parents have higher levels of anxiety and depression than those without children. I don't dispute those studies at all. The question, though, is, why is there such anxiety, such sadness, in the lives of parents?

I hope I don't succumb to the sin of anxiety or lack of trust in God. But I do worry about my sons. I hope for the best for them. I feel the weight of my example before them. Before I became a father, I felt conviction of sin when I snapped at someone, but I never felt the depression that comes with realizing that I've snapped at one of *my sons*. I feel sorry for a young man who's been rejected by the woman he thought was meant to be his wife, but I've never cried about it. I can imagine myself weeping behind closed doors, though, if it ever happened to my son Timothy. I've always loathed child molesters and raged against the way the courts and churches so often coddle them. But I've never had my blood pressure accelerate the way it does when a socially awkward, creepily friendly man kneels to talk to my kids. Having a baby yanks one into a whole new world of responsibility for the shaping of a life, a family, a future.

That kind of anxiety isn't limited to parents within a household. We can also see the same thing in the "fathers" and "mothers" within the church, those who love the gathered believers with a love that cherishes, and aches, like that of a parent.

The apostle Paul writes of his "toil . . . night and day" over the church at Thessalonica because he loved them "like a nursing mother taking care of her own children" (1 Thess. 2:7–9). One can sense the gravity of emotion when the apostle John warns the churches with the urgency of a father, "Little children, keep yourselves from idols" (1 John 5:21)—just like a mom who calls out, "Johnny! Stay away from that electrical wire!"

It's easy, though, not to feel this. A certain kind of manufactured calm can come to those who don't wish to be parents or who abandon their children to the welfare state or to the abortionist's sword. This kind of freedom doesn't startle you out of a midnight slumber or cause you to run anxious hands through your hair in frustration. No one is watching to see how you trained up a new generation to worship or spurn the God of your fathers.

But what an impoverished sense of pseudo-*shalom* this must be. It's the peace of a beggar who is content to glean from the fields while never risking the possibility of failing as a farmer. There's a high price for such peace.

Every night I lay my hands on the head of my four sons and pray for the salvation of Benjamin, Timothy, Samuel, and Jonah. I pray they'll be godly men of courage and conviction. I pray God will give them godly wives (one apiece) and that he would spare them from rebellious teenage years and from the horror of divorce.

And when I'm really aware of my responsibility, I pray they'll be good dads. Yes, I pray for the salvation of the world, for healed marriages across the board. But not like this. They're my boys. And sometimes when I think about the alternative to their salvation, there's a sawing ache I never knew as a single man looking at a world map. There's a sense of my own helplessness—and my own possible failure—that never kept me awake at night in a college dormitory room.

I guess you could call that burden depressing—sometimes it is. I suppose you could track it on a chart as anxiety. And I suppose you could avoid that depression, that anxiety, by seeking to feed only your own mouth, to be held responsible for only your own life, or just yours and a spouse's. But what if in so doing, you're protecting yourself from more than possible sadness and grief? What if you're protecting yourself from love?

God is not anxious. God isn't depressed. But God's fatherhood is pictured for us as a tumultuous, fighting kind of fatherhood—the kind that rips open the seas and drowns armies. Joseph probably had no idea that he was a living reenactment of the deliverance of Israel from Egypt. He probably never thought about the fact he was serving as an icon of his God. He just did what seemed right, in obedience to the Word of God. But he was participating in something dramatic—in every sense of the word.

When we adopt—and when we encourage a culture of adoption in our churches and communities—we're picturing something that's true about our God. We, like Jesus, see what our Father is doing and do likewise (John 5:19). And what our Father is doing, it turns out, is fighting for orphans, making them sons and daughters.

ADOPTION AND THE WALK OF FAITH

Our contemporary cartoonish, two-dimensional picture of Joseph too easily ignores how difficult it was for him to do what he did. Imagine for a minute that one of the teenagers in your church were to stand up behind the pulpit to give her testimony. She's eight months pregnant and unmarried. After a few minutes of talking about God's working in her life and about how excited she is to be a mother, she starts talking about how thankful she is that she's remained sexually pure, kept all the "True Love Waits" commitments she made in her youth group Bible study, and is glad to announce that she's still a virgin. You'd immediately conclude that the girl's either delusional or lying.

When contemporary biblical revisionists scoff at the virgin birth of Jesus and other miracles, they often tell us we're now beyond such "myths" since we live in a post-Enlightenment, scientifically progressive information age. What such critics miss is the fact that virgin conceptions have always seemed ridiculous. People in first-century Palestine knew how babies were conceived. The implausibility of the whole thing is evident in the biblical text itself. When Mary tells Joseph she is pregnant, his first reaction isn't a cheery "It's beginning to look a lot like Christmas." No, he assumes what any of us would conclude was going on, and he sets out to end their betrothal.

But then God enters the scene.

When God speaks in a dream to Joseph about the identity of Jesus, Joseph, like everyone who follows Christ, recognizes the voice and goes forward (Matt. 1:21–24). Joseph's adoption and protection of Jesus is simply the outworking of that belief.

In believing God, Joseph probably walks away from his reputation. The wags in his hometown would probably always whisper about how "poor Joseph was hoodwinked by that girl" or how "old Joseph got himself in trouble with that girl." As the stakes get higher, Joseph certainly walks away from his economic security. In first-century Galilee, after all, one doesn't simply move to Egypt, the way one might today decide to move to New York or London. Joseph surrenders a household economy, a vocation probably built up over generations, handed down to him, one would suppose, by his father.

Again, Joseph was unique in one sense. None of us will ever be called to be father to God. But in another very real sense, Joseph's faith was exactly the same as ours. The letter of James, for instance, speaks of the definition of faith in this way: "Religion that is pure and undefiled before God, the Father, is this: to visit orphans and widows in their affliction, and to keep oneself unstained from the world" (1:27). James is the one who tells us further that faith is not mere intellectual belief, the faith of demons (2:19), but is instead a faith that works.

James shows us that Abraham's belief is seen in his offering up Isaac, knowing God would keep his promise and raise him from the dead (2:21–23). We know Rahab has faith not simply because she raises her hand in agreement with the Hebrew spies but because in hiding them from the enemy she is showing she trusts God to save her (2:25). James tells us that genuine faith shelters the orphan.

What gives even more weight to these words is the identity of the human author. This letter is written by James of the Jerusalem church, the brother of our Lord Jesus.[4] How much of this "pure and undefiled religion" did James see first in the life of his own earthly father? Did the image of Joseph linger in James's mind as he inscribed the words of an orphan-protecting, living faith?

Not long ago I sat in a coffee shop with a friend and former student, now a faithful pastor, hearing how things were moving along in his congregation. He talked about various mission projects within the church, including a yearly mission trip to an overseas orphanage to care for the children there and to help connect them with adopting parents. Some folks in the church, my pastor friend said, wanted to discontinue the orphanage work in order to do something, as they put it, "more evangelistic." A group of faithful Christians have been serving orphans—helping place them in Christian homes where they'll grow up with the gospel—and some feel guilty for not doing something "evangelistic"! That's a tragedy. What better way is there to bring the good news of Christ than to see his unwanted little brothers and sisters placed in families where they'll be raised in the nurture and admonition of the Lord?

Because genuine faith is orphan-protecting, a culture of adoption and a culture of evangelism coexist together. Indeed they grow from the same root. Christians who counsel pregnant women and who staff orphanages and who help families adopt aren't "social welfare people" as opposed to the "soul-winning people" in the next pew.

A few years ago, the Presiding Bishop of the Episcopal Church USA kicked up a stir of controversy with comments in a national

---

[4]For a detailed discussion of the identity of James and his relationship to Jesus, see Douglas J. Moo, *The Letter of James,* Pillar New Testament Commentary (Grand Rapids, MI: Eerdmans, 2000), 11–22. I agree with Moo's assessment that the author of the letter of James is indeed our Lord's brother, per the traditional view.

newsmagazine, differentiating mainline Episcopalians from more theologically conservative groups such as Roman Catholics and evangelical Protestants. In her view, Episcopalians "tend to be better educated and tend to reproduce at lower rates than some other denominations." Episcopalians, she said, "encourage people to pay attention to the stewardship of the earth and not use more than their portion."[5]

Well, she's right, of course. Mainline Episcopalians in this country do tend to be well-educated and affluent, and the homeschooling mom with six kids in tow in the line at the grocery store in front of you is not likely to be an Episcopalian. But what about those "other denominations" the bishop mentioned? What about those of us whose communions are less well-educated and who have, as she put it, "theological reasons for producing lots of children"?

My denomination was once seen as one of the most aggressively evangelistic groups on the planet. Some of you may have similar stories about your denominations and churches, and maybe you've seen the same kind of trajectory. In my grandfather's day, conservative evangelicals were often derided by American culture as redneck and backward. There's still hostility toward evangelical Christianity in certain sectors of American life, of course, but evangelical Christians are now invited to the Rotary Club meetings. We're being elected to Congress. People now at least pretend to know how to respond to our evangelistic tracts in order to get our votes for President of the United States. We're not in the trailer parks anymore. Our young men are successful, suburban, and career-minded—and our young women are too. Like the rest of American culture, we often see children as something expected but to be minimized, lest they get in the way of our dreams. And we think that's a sign of health.

Meanwhile our baptisms go down, and our birthrates do too. It turns out that keeping up with the Episcopalians can have a downside.

[5]Deborah Solomon, "State of the Church: Questions for Katharine Jefferts Schori," *New York Times Magazine*, November 19, 2006, 21.

Churches that don't celebrate children aren't going to celebrate evangelism. After all, the "be fruitful and multiply" clause in Genesis is echoed in the Great Commission of Jesus (Matt. 28:16–20), a mission that also seeks to fill the entire earth. Jesus links procreation to new creation by speaking of new converts as newborn babies and of conversion itself as a new birth. When Jesus stands before his Father with the redeemed of all the ages, he will announce us as "the children God has given me" (Heb. 2:13).

Churches that mimic (even if by default, with silence) the culture's view that life is about possessions or sentimental pop-music romance or self-advancement simply aren't going to produce men and women committed to giving up these things for the cause of global evangelism and missions. Faithful Christian congregations must be distinct from the blob spirituality of contemporary Western civilization. And what is more countercultural than the embrace of children as gifts from a good Lord? We live in an era when a mom with five children receives snide comments, even from her children's pediatrician ("Don't you know what's causing that?"). A congregation that exults in new life, from the pulpit and from the pew, is a congregation that's going to cause onlookers to ask why.

If the people in our congregation become other-directed instead of self-directed in the adoption of unwanted children, they are going to be other-directed instead of self-directed in their verbal witness to people in their community. On the other hand, the same self-interest that sears over the joy of birth will sear over the joy of the new birth. The numbness to earthly adoption is easily translated to numbness to spiritual adoption. But if people in our churches learn not to grumble at the blessing of minivans filled with children—some of whom don't look anything alike—they're going to learn not to grumble at the blessing of a congregation filling with new people, some of whom don't look anything alike. If our churches learn to rejoice in newness of life in the church nursery, they'll more easily rejoice at newness of life in the church baptistery, and vice versa.

This doesn't mean that we should equate fertility (or prolific adoption) with spirituality. God calls many believers not to marry so that, like the apostle Paul, they can devote themselves totally to Great Commission service. Others will not be blessed with large families or, as we'll discuss in the next chapter, with children at all. We must insist on the church as a household, not as a collection of family units. But at the same time, can't we insist that our view of children be dictated by the book of Proverbs rather than by Madison Avenue or Wall Street?

Unbridled capitalist prosperity doesn't make love, babies, or societies. It certainly doesn't build a church. What we need is a vision that transcends our gnawing after what we think we want and need. We need a vision that shows us that a person's life "does not consist in the abundance of his possessions" (Luke 12:15).

Seeking first the kingdom of God, as Jesus tells us to do (Matt. 6:33), means recognizing what kind of kingdom we're seeking. When we pray "Your kingdom come," we're asking that "your will be done, on earth as it is in heaven" (Matt. 6:10). When the psalmist cries out for that kingdom to come, he pleads, "Give justice to the weak and the fatherless; maintain the right of the afflicted and the destitute" (Ps. 82:3).

The kingdom of Christ is characterized in Scripture as a kingdom of rescued children. Solomon looks to the final reign of God's anointed and sings, "For he delivers the needy when he calls, the poor and him who has no helper. He has pity on the weak and the needy, and saves the lives of the needy. From oppression and violence he redeems their life, and precious is their blood in his sight" (Ps. 72:12–14). When we protect and welcome children, we're announcing something about Jesus and his kingdom.

If that characterizes the kingdom to come, then why aren't our churches—which are, after all, outposts of that rule of Jesus— characterized by it now? When we recognize the face of Jesus reflected in faces we may never see until the resurrection—those of the vulnerable unborn and unwanted—we're doing more than cultural activism. We are contending for the faith once for all delivered to the saints (Jude 3).

An orphan-protecting adoption culture is countercultural—and always has been. Some of the earliest records we have of the Christian churches speak of how Christians, remarkably, protected children in the face of a culture of death pervasive in the Roman Empire. The followers of Jesus, though, did not kill their offspring, even when it would have made economic or social sense to do so.[6] This is still distinctively Christian in a world that increasingly sees children as, at best, a commodity to be controlled and, at worst, a nuisance to be contained. Think of how revolutionary it is for Christians to adopt a young boy with a cleft palate from a region of India where most people see him as "defective." Think of how counterintuitive it is for Christians to adopt a Chinese girl—when many there see her as a disappointment. Think of how odd it must seem to American secularists to see Christians adopting a baby whose body trembles with an addiction to the cocaine her mother sent through her bloodstream before birth. Think of the kind of credibility such action lends to the proclamation of our gospel.

An adoption culture in our churches advances the cause of life, even beyond the individual lives of the children adopted. Imagine if Christian churches were known as the places where unwanted babies become beloved children. If this were the case across the board around the world, sure, there would still be abortions, there would still be abusive homes. But wouldn't we see more women willing to give their children life if they'd seen with their own eyes what an adoption culture looks like? And wouldn't these mothers and fathers, who may themselves feel unwanted, be a bit more ready to hear our talk about a kingdom where all are welcomed?

The contemporary Planned Parenthood movement was started by a woman named Margaret Sanger, who defended abortion rights on the basis of eugenics, the search for "good genes" based on the

---

[6]"The Epistle to Diognetus," in *The Apostolic Fathers: Greek Texts and English Translations*, 3rd ed., trans. Michael W. Holmes (Grand Rapids, MI: Baker, 2007), 703.

racist and evolutionary notions of "social Darwinism" prevalent in her day. Sanger's grandson, Alexander, continues her viewpoint, updated with contemporary notions of sociobiology, in virulent opposition to the viability of an adoption culture—on Darwinist grounds. "Adoption is counter-intuitive from an evolutionary vantage point of both the biological mother and the adoptive parents," Sanger argues. "Adoption requires a person to devote time and resources to raising a child that is not genetically related. Adoption puts the future of a child in the control of a stranger."[7] It's easier for a woman to have an abortion, Sanger argues, or for a family to refuse to think about adopting because evolution and biology "conspire to thwart adoption. Evolution has programmed women to be nurturers of the children they bear."[8] That's why, the abortion industry heir contends, adoption "as the 'solution' to the abortion problem is a cruel hoax."[9]

Sanger has an ideology, a family heritage, and the financial viability of the abortion industry to guard; so his words aren't going to convince many followers of Jesus. But aren't they sad, and telling?

Perhaps what our churches need most of all in our defense of the faith against Darwinian despair is not more resources on how the fossil record fits with the book of Genesis and not more arguments on how molecular structures show evidence of design. Perhaps the most practical way your congregation can show Darwinism to be wrong is to showcase families for whom love is more than gene protection.

As with Joseph, this orphan-protecting faith is personal as well as corporate. At the Judgment Seat of Christ, all of us will be evaluated as to the authenticity of our faith on the basis of our reaction to "the least of these" (Matt. 25:31–46). At first blush, this looks like works-righteousness, the very kind of thing away from which the rest of the Bible is calling us. You might wonder, if we're judged on this basis,

---

[7]Alexander Sanger, *Beyond Choice: Reproductive Freedom in the 21st Century* (New York: PublicAffairs, 2004), 142.
[8]Ibid., 143.
[9]Ibid., 144.

then shouldn't each of us adopt as many children as we have square footage in our homes—and then buy more square footage? No. The remarkable thing about Jesus' revelation about the Judgment Seat is that neither the "sheep" (those who inherit the kingdom) nor the "goats" (those who inherit hell) seem to know what Jesus is talking about. When Jesus tells the righteous they sheltered and fed and clothed him in his distress, they ask, "Lord, when did we . . ." (Matt. 25:37). And when Jesus tells the unrighteous they refused to do such things, they also ask, "Lord, when did we . . ." (Matt. 25:44).

At issue isn't a list of righteous deeds. At issue is whether Jesus knows us, whether we are "blessed" by the Father (Matt. 25:34). The faith that sees Christ presented in the gospel sees Christ in his brothers when they appear providentially in the life of the believer. Jesus tells us there'll always be people who appeal to their knowledge of the King, their "personal relationship to Jesus." Do they recognize him, though, apart from his sky-exploding glory? Do they see the covert Christ in the suffering of the vulnerable?

Not every believer will stand praying outside an abortion clinic. Not every believer will take a pregnant teenager into his or her guest bedroom. Not every believer is called to adopt children. But every believer is called to recognize Jesus in the face of his little brothers and sisters when he decides to show up in their lives, even if it interrupts everything else.

The judgment of this kind of faith is intensely personal. A few years ago a group of us were riveted as we listened to Billy Graham at a crusade in Indianapolis preaching on final judgment. The evangelist told the crowd that many of them mistakenly thought of the judgment to come in the same way they think of the Indianapolis 500 car race—as a great mass of people milling around together. "You think you'll be there with all your friends, drinking beer," Graham said. "But you're wrong. When you stand in judgment, you'll stand *alone*." The evangelist was old and weak. His voice was shaky, and he had to be helped to the podium, hardly the fiery preacher of the mid-twentieth century. But when the crowd heard the word *alone*, in that famous Carolina mountain accent, there was almost a chill in the stadium. In the judgment to come, our faith will lie exposed before the eyes of our God, and there will be nowhere to hide.

Thousands of years ago, a man named Job recognized that his own judgment would have to do with his treatment of orphans. In the book of Job, the suffering man told God that he would neither withhold food or raise his hand against the fatherless (Job 31:16–22). Job said instead that "from my youth the fatherless grew up with me as with a father, and from my mother's womb I guided the widow" (Job 31:18). Why was this so? Job said, "For I was in terror of calamity from God, and I could not have faced his majesty" (Job 31:23).

Joseph of Nazareth could resonate with Job's plea. Joseph easily could have walked out to the city gates, shaking his head to his friends. "You'll never believe the crazy dream I had last night." He no doubt would have denounced everywhere Herod's pagan insanity in killing babies and toddlers. No one would have blamed him for putting aside his betrothal to Mary. In fact, he probably would have been praised at his funeral for his kindness in not calling for her to be stoned to death. Joseph could have married a pious Jewish woman, could have fathered several of his "own" children. He could have slept easily at night, perhaps, and then died an old man. No one would have thought him to be evil or even negligent. But if he'd done that, he would have been standing with the spirit of antichrist rather than with the Spirit of Christ. No one else was called to adopt this Christ-child, but he was. And because he believed his God, he obeyed him, even to his own hurt.

Joseph's faith was the same kind of faith that saves us. Very few, if any, of us will have a dream directing us to adopt a child. None of us will be directed to do what Joseph did—to teach Jesus Christ how to saw through wood or to recite Deuteronomy in Hebrew. But all of us are called to be compassionate. All of us are called to remember the poor. All of us are called to remember the fatherless and the widows. That will look different in our different lives, with the different situations and resources God has given us. But for all of us there'll be a judgment to test the genuineness of our faith. And for some of us, there'll be some orphan faces there.

CONCLUSION

It's a shame that Joseph is so neglected in our thoughts and affections, even at Christmastime. If we pay attention to him, though, we just might see a model for a new generation of Christians. We might see how to live as the presence of Christ in a culture of death. We might see how to image a protective Father, how to preach a life-affirming gospel, even in a culture captivated by the spirit of Herod.

If we follow in the way of Joseph, perhaps we'll see a battalion of new church-sponsored clinics for pregnant women in crisis situations (and I word it this way because, as a dear friend rightly reminds me, there are no "crisis pregnancies"). Perhaps we'll train God-called women in our churches to counsel confused young women, counselors able and equipped to provide an alternative to the slick but deadly propaganda of the abortion profiteers. If we walk in Joseph's way, perhaps we'll see pastors who will prophetically call on Christians to oppose the death culture by rescuing babies and children through adoption.

Think of the plight of the orphan somewhere right now out there in the world. It's not just that she's lonely. It's that she has no inheritance, no future. With every passing year, she's less "cute," less adoptable. In just a few years, on her eighteenth birthday, she'll be expelled from the orphanage or from "the system." What will happen to her then? Maybe she'll join the military or find some job training. Maybe she'll stare at a tile on the ceiling above her as her body is violated by a man who's willing to pay her enough to eat for a day, alone in a back alley or in front of a camera crew of strangers. Maybe she'll place a revolver in her mouth or tie a rope around her neck, knowing no one will have to deal with her except, once again, the bureaucratic "authorities" who can clean up the mess she leaves behind. Can you feel the force of such desperation? Jesus can. She's his little sister.

What if a mighty battalion of Christian parents would open their hearts and their homes to unwanted infants—infants some so-called "clinics" would like to see carried out with the medical waste? It might mean that next Christmas there'll be one more stocking at the chimney at your house—a new son or daughter who escaped the abortionist's knife or the orphanage's grip to find at your knee the grace of a carpenter's Son.

Planned Parenthood thinks "Choice on Earth" is the message of Christmas, and perhaps it is in a Christmas culture more identified with shopping malls than with churches. But we know better, or at least we should. Let's follow the footsteps of the other man at the manger, the quiet one. And as we read the proclamation of the shepherds, exploding in the sky as a declaration of war, let's remind a miserable generation there are some things more joyous than choice—things like peace and life and love.

4

Don't You Want Your Own Kids?

How to Know If You—or Someone You Love—
Should Consider Adoption

IT WAS CRUMPLED UP, lying there behind a stack of yellowing magazines and some picture frames. It was a little blue denim baseball hat, with some embroidered ladybugs on it. The blueness of it made it acceptable for wear by a little boy, the ladybugs for a girl, I guess. I sat there and unfolded it in my hands, smoothing away the wrinkles from the fabric. I'd put it there a long time ago.

I remember the day that hat arrived in the mail—by special delivery along with a large flowering plant and a card from my parents. My wife Maria was pregnant—at long last—and my parents were giddy with anticipation. I had called about an upcoming family wedding and, having rehearsed my words over and over, asked my parents whether they thought our relative would mind if Maria and I brought a guest. "Not a problem!" they both said, then asked who our guest would be. "Well, that's just it," I said. "I don't know. I don't even know if it'll be a 'he' or a 'she.' The guest will be our baby son or daughter." They squealed with glee. When the package arrived, we set the plant in the corner of our apartment living room, where the sun could get to it, and I placed the little hat on the bookshelf in the same room. Every day we'd look at it and imagine it bouncing along on the head of our little child.

We didn't expect to hear the words we'd hear from a technician at the obstetrician's office. As she waved the wand over Maria's stomach to hear the heartbeat of our baby, she suddenly stopped her small talk. "Have you had any spotting?" she asked. Immediately I knew what had happened, and the doctor soon confirmed it. Our baby was, in his icily clinical wording, a "blighted ovum." Maria had suffered a miscarriage.

I don't think I'd ever really understood the biblical imagery of Rachel weeping for her children "because they are no more" (Jer. 31:15) until that minute. We were both inconsolable, plunged into a depression of punctured expectation and plunging adrenaline. When we walked into our tiny apartment from the doctor's office, Maria went directly upstairs to bed. I walked over to the shelf and grabbed that little blue hat, stuffing it into a cabinet. I didn't want Maria to have to see it. But I couldn't throw it away.

In time, Maria became pregnant again—and miscarried again, and then yet again. I feared we were staring into an abyss of being an elderly couple all alone, like some of the people we'd known as children. Those older, childless couples didn't really know how to speak to children, so they'd talk about the weather and how their tomato plants were doing; they started keeping scrapbooks with pictures of their cats. I hated cats. But was that our future?

For a long time I'd find myself slipping into a Christian bookstore near my work. There was a listening booth where one could "sample" albums for sale in the store. I would, almost compulsively, go in and listen to one song, "Thought You'd Be Here" by the artist Wes King, which includes the repeating line, "We thought you'd be here by now." My eyes would fill with tears at one particular point in the song, when the musical atmosphere grows grave and King sings, "I never knew the silence could make me so deaf / I never knew that I could miss someone I haven't met."[1] I didn't buy that song. I couldn't bring myself to have the music in my house or in my car. But I wanted to hear it. It seemed as though this singer was the only one who knew what this felt like. It was like missing someone—kind of like the feeling I'd have for my parents when I'd go away as a child

---

[1]"Thought You'd Be Here," written and performed by Wes King, on the album *A Room Full of Stories*, Sparrow Records, 1997.

to a relative's house for a week or so, kind of like the feeling I had for my wife-to-be when I'd moved an hour away from her when we were engaged. It was a homesickness, missing someone whose face I couldn't picture. All I could see in my imagination was a blurred little face with a blue denim hat on top.

Maybe you're in a similar situation. Maybe you keep getting blank pregnancy tests, or maybe there's been pregnancy after pregnancy that never comes to term. Maybe a doctor has told you it doesn't look very likely that you'll ever be a parent. Maybe the second and third opinions have been the same. Maybe you wouldn't want me, or anyone, to know it, but you really don't want to adopt—at least not now, at least not until you've given it every shot to deliver a child biologically. What should you do?

Or maybe you love somebody in that situation, and you really don't know what to say. You've been told it's uncaring to suggest adoption, especially if you have children. So how do you help your friend or family member, with Christlike compassion and wisdom?

Or perhaps you're in the exact opposite situation. Maybe the Lord's blessed you with a child—or even a house bustling with children. Maybe you feel a desire, perhaps even a calling, to adopt a child, but you're not sure if you should. Why should you adopt, you might wonder, when there are so many childless couples out there who would love to have a baby? Would it be right to have an "adopted child" right along with your "biological children," or would that psychologically assault all of them?

The Holy Spirit didn't breathe out the pages ahead. They instead represent a word of counsel to those of you in each of the situations above—and those of you who may find yourselves later in one of those situations. If you disagree with me on any of these points, well, that's okay by me.

I want to say some things to you I wish I'd had someone say to me when I was confused in the face of blank pregnancy tests and miscarried babies. I want to express some things I wish I'd known before I had four children, half of whom are labeled "adopted" and half of whom are labeled "biological." I want to remind you—all of you—what our God said to weeping Rachel: "There is hope for your future, declares the LORD, and your children shall come back to their own country" (Jer. 31:17).

CONSIDERING ADOPTION FOR THOSE WHO ARE (OR FEAR THEY MIGHT BE) INFERTILE

I could tell she was nervous. She laughed a little too easily, a little too mechanically, kind of like an animated Eskimo in the Disney World "It's a Small World" ride. Her husband was calm, a little too calm, patting his wife's knee and speaking in a soothing, almost therapist-like voice. We didn't know them well, but they'd asked to visit that night to talk about infertility. They'd known Maria and I had lived through years of it, and they wanted to seek our advice about reproductive technology. The doctors they were seeing had given up on the more routine infertility treatments and were now counseling some extreme measures, such as in vitro fertilization or artificial insemination. They were worried, it became clear as we sipped coffee and ate banana pudding, about the cost.

"Why don't you adopt?" I said. "For the amount of money the doctors are asking for with this, you could adopt two children. And you wouldn't have the risk of continually failed treatments." The wife's eyes darted back and forth from her husband to her coffee cup.

"Well," she said. "We'd love to adopt . . . you know, someday. We think it's a great thing. But first we want to have our own kids. I am happy to adopt, but I want that first baby to be mine." The husband followed up, elaborating on what she'd said. They loved the idea of adoption, but they really wanted to be able to see their own eyes staring up at them in the face of their child. I put down my coffee cup and leaned forward.

"So, here's the question," I asked. "Do you want most of all to be parents, or do you want most of all to be conservators of your genetic material?"

Maria fidgeted in her chair, giving me the look that means, "Are you going to be this rude to our guests?" She was right. I felt the liberty to be so blunt, however, because I'd had almost the exact same thought process this couple had, and I'd wished I'd had someone there to pop me on the jaw. I knew the fear in their faces because I'd seen it in mine. But I also knew the joy they were bypassing because I almost passed it up too.

If you're infertile—or if you're counseling someone who is—the first thing you should know is that the sadness you feel is normal. In fact, it's holy. As we've seen, God delights in fruitfulness, and in children. The marriage union, the apostle Paul tell us, is a copy—a copy of the mystery of Christ's union with his church (Eph. 5:22–33). That union brings forth fruit; it incarnates its love in children, "a great multitude that no one could number" (Rev. 7:9).

Barrenness is part of the curse. By this I mean it's not part of the original creation that our God blessed as "very good" (Gen. 1:31). As God was bringing the Israelites into the Promised Land, he promised his people he would bless them, if they were obedient, with every blessing, including "the fruit of your womb" (Deut. 28:11). Maybe you're infertile and you're wondering if this means you're personally cursed by God. Maybe you read passages in the Old Testament about the blessing of a fruitful womb for the obedient and the curses of barrenness for the cursed, and you're wondering if you're rejected by God.

No.

Remember, we can't bypass Jesus when reading passages that he tells us are all about him (Luke 24:44–45). He is the obedient Israel, and he receives the blessing of God. He is also the One who bore the curse on our behalf, every bit of it (Gal. 3:13). If you've believed in Christ, you are blessed and not cursed, whatever the situation you see around you.

I can't explain what the infertility means for you, but I can tell you that God is not punishing you. How do I know? If you are in Christ, your punishment was absorbed in the body of a crucified Jesus. There is no more condemnation for you (Rom. 8:1). God is discipling you, shaping you, and he often uses suffering to do so, but he isn't punishing you. He views you within the body of his Christ, and he loves and delights in you. Whatever is happening in your life, nothing can separate you from the love of God in Christ (Rom. 8:31–39). If neither death nor life, nor angels, nor rulers, nor things present, nor things to come can sever you from God's love, can the rhythms and silences of your reproductive organs do so?

So, what if you're not sure if you're a follower of Jesus or if you know you don't believe all these claims of "good news"? Might it be that the infertility is God's getting at you for your lack of faith? God has told us how he deals with sinners, and this isn't it. As a matter of fact, the Bible is filled with righteous people crying out to God as to why he lets the wicked prosper. You've seen that guy you know is cheating on his wife pushing the stroller down the sidewalk. Prostitutes and slumlords and child molesters all become pregnant or have children. That isn't a sign of God's approval of their lives, and your infertility isn't a sign of God's disfavor.

As a matter of fact, as we've seen earlier, if you don't know Christ, God is not disciplining you at all (Heb. 12:8), though he is sovereign over everything that happens in your life. He is calling you to be found in Christ, and the curse that awaits you comes at judgment, not now. For now there's a temporary suspension of doom, and God is doing good to you, as you can see by the air you're breathing and the blood pushing through your veins (Acts 14:16–17). As Jesus tells his disciples, the horrible circumstances that happen to people in this life aren't a one-to-one retaliation for sin (Luke 13:1–4). But Jesus does tell us that if we don't repent, these things—be it infertility or towers falling on us—will be the least of our problems.

Jesus rebukes his disciples' assumptions that a man born blind is being particularly punished, either for his sin or for that of his parents (John 9:1–3). Jesus recognizes, though, that blindness is not good; it is part of a universe in which God's reign is not yet realized. It's right to be sad about infertility. That's why God so often in Scripture hears the prayers of barren women.

Think about Hannah, the wife of Elkanah. "She was," the Bible tells us, "deeply distressed and prayed to the LORD and wept bitterly" (1 Sam. 1:10). She sees herself as afflicted and even refuses to eat in her sadness. She is not pictured as unfaithful—far from it. Instead, the Bible pictures Hannah as driven to exactly the kind of prayer we mentioned earlier—groaning too deep for words through the Holy Spirit (Rom. 8:23, 26). Her groaning is so deep, as a matter of fact, that she's mistaken for a drunk (1 Sam. 1:12–15), something that happens again later on in Scripture when the Holy Spirit touches down among the people of God (Acts 2:13–15). Hannah, along with a host of other childless families in Scripture, is sad, and such sadness isn't wrong.

The second thing you should know, whether you think you might be infertile or if you're counseling someone who is, is that the situation isn't as dire as you think. God delights in answering prayers for children. Hannah's prayer, you'll remember, was heard. The psalmist sang out:

> *Who is like the LORD our God,*
> *   who is seated on high,*
> *who looks far down*
> *   on the heavens and the earth?*
> *He raises the poor from the dust*
> *   and lifts the needy from the ash heap,*
> *to make them sit with princes,*
> *   with the princes of his people.*
> *He gives the barren woman a home,*
> *   making her the joyous mother of children.*
> *Praise the LORD! (Ps. 113:5–9)*

Once, after one of the miscarriages, my wife came downstairs to find me crying on the couch in our living room. After pretending to be the strong protector/provider for a long time, I just gurgled forth, "I am just realizing that I'm going to be an old man with no kids, that I'm going to die alone, and that's the worst thing I can imagine." My wife says those words stabbed right through her, and they reverberated through her memory for years: ". . . the worst thing I can imagine." To her it sounded like, "I'm sorry I married you," which was the furthest thing from what I meant. Those words were extraordinarily hurtful because they reinforced the "performance anxiety" she already felt as she tried to conceive. She wondered every time she saw that single line on the pregnancy test, "What's wrong with me?" and now she thought I was asking that too. Her body had become, it seemed to her, her enemy, and now it was mine as well, she concluded.

Chances are, someone you know feels that way right now. Maybe you will one day, though you can't imagine it right now. What I wish I'd known then is how God enjoys answering prayers for children. I am not saying that God grants children to everyone who is infertile, as in some kind of "word faith" aberrant theology. I am saying, though, that I have never met anyone who wanted children who did not eventually have them—through birth or through adoption. I know there are couples who don't ever have children but who don't in anguish long for them. I know some couples like that. I'm sure there must be people who die lonely, wanting and praying for children all the while. In this time-between-the-times, there are unanswered prayers and horrible things that happen. But I've never seen anyone personally in that situation.

When it comes to pregnancy, it seems, even more obviously than in other situations, those who ask tend to (eventually) receive, and those who seek tend to find (although perhaps not in the way they first intended). Your prayers are not accidental, after all. If you are walking in step with the Spirit, he intercedes for you, to bring your prayers into conformity with God's will for your Christ-conformity (Rom. 8:26). This doesn't mean that your praying for children means you'll be granted children, but it does mean that if you're praying for God's will to be done and you find yourself continually seeking to pray for children, perhaps God is readying you for children. This means your number one priority as you wait for God's answer is to pursue holiness. Embed yourself in the life of your church; worship, love, utilize your spiritual gifts; be a spiritual mother or father to someone in need.

Your situation if you're infertile is probably not as hopeless as you think. Your friend's situation, if you're ministering to someone infertile, probably feels far more hopeless to him or to her than you can imagine.

Infertility isn't hopeless, but it is dangerous. If you're grappling with a so-far unanswered plea for children, let me stop and warn you about something. Remember that your life is being lived out in a world that's more than what you can see. You bear the image of God, you resemble Jesus, and so you are a target for demonic principalities and powers who seek to turn your affections away from your Lord. Every one of us has weak points sized up by these rebel forces, and your struggle with infertility is no exception.

It's easy to become bitter, envious, and covetous when you want children and fear you can't have them. Moses tells us this is precisely what happened to our foremother Rachel when she wanted children desperately while her sister had them easily (Gen. 30:1). You can find yourself snapping at the supermarket clerk who asks if you have children, as though she asked what you look like naked. It's easy to refuse to attend your best friend's baby shower because you wish you were having one yourself. You likewise can easily shut down your emotional life as much as possible, numbing yourself to keep from getting hurt further.

If you find yourself mistrusting God's goodness to you or caving introspectively in on yourself or unable to rejoice with those who rejoice and to weep with those who weep, recognize what's happening—and that it isn't good. There are many, many infertile persons who don't have any such struggles, but I did, and there are many who do. The most perilous aspect of this is the fact that very few of your friends will call you on it. Your best friend may withstand you to your face if he or she hears you brag about yourself or mistreat your mom or boast about the great pornography you viewed last night. But, except in the most exceptional of circumstances, he or she will be reluctant to say anything about sin that seems bound up with infertility. If your friends aren't or haven't been in that situation, they'll feel cold and heartless by bringing any of it up.

That puts you in a very vulnerable situation, a situation—if you give in to it—that adoption or pregnancy can't undo. Be sure, before you assess any of your options, to discern—through self-evaluation, prayer, and counsel from godly pastors and friends—what kind of spiritual collateral damage is being done on your affections and conscience by your life situation. If it's little or none, rejoice with gratitude. If it's significant, seek repentance and God's favor to overcome it—and then proceed toward your goal.

The special toll that infertility can take on humans, who are designed to welcome children, also means that infertile couples are often reluctant to think about adoption, at least at first. The couple I mentioned before, in my living room, said they felt as though adoption was "long-term babysitting." That's a common sentiment, one that I shared myself at the beginning. Adoption seems to many infertile couples (including Christians) to be a second-best option for those who can't in any other way have children "of our own."

Now, again, this desire to become pregnant and to bear children is natural and holy (1 Tim. 2:15). It's also godly to love our own flesh and blood (Gen. 2:23; Eph. 5:29), which is why God designed the one-flesh union and human procreation the way he did. But, like all other human desires and affections, this can be twisted into idolatry.

That's always been true, but never truer than now when human biology is big business. Often Christians struggling with infertility find themselves up against a hard sell from their doctors to pursue expensive and ethically problematic reproductive technologies. Sometimes these doctors are operating from a motive of compassion. They just want to see these hurting couples have what they want so badly—a baby. And we have the technology available in many cases to see to it that this happens.

Often, though, doctors and scientists are working from a Darwinian starting point—that biological relatedness is the alpha and omega of familial love. One of the most infamous advocates for human cloning in the world today dismisses adoption as a solution for infertility because, he argues, human beings are evolutionarily hard-wired to "complete their life cycle" through passing on their genetic material.

If Darwinian naturalism is true, then adoption makes little sense, whatever technologies are available. Then again, if Darwinian naturalism is true, then let us eat, drink, and be merry, for tomorrow we die. Christian advocacy for adoption challenges the reigning worldview from a perspective that strikes Darwinian concepts of the family at their very core. Grounded in a multinational, multi-tribal church as the unified Body of Christ, a biblical vision of adoption sees beyond the stilted utopianism of "designer children" and our own genetic idolatry. That's sometimes hard to see though, from either side of the doctor's desk.

Additionally, like a dentist who sees potential crowns on every set of teeth, some less scrupulous doctors have a distinct financial incentive to see couples spend thousands upon thousands of dollars on extensive reproductive technologies rather than on adoption.

Couples who think they might be infertile need to take warning here. It doesn't matter what one's convictions are about Christian ethics and about the limits of what one should do in "getting a baby" because given the right circumstances, you can talk yourself into anything. We might let a teenage boy sleep in a tent with a teenage girl at youth camp, saying to ourselves, "I asked, and both of them believe fornication is a sin." But in the desperate desire of the moment, both of them will redefine their convictions, their situation, and what they're doing in order to get what they want. All of us, sadly, are like this. If you're desperate enough to be a parent, you'll convince yourself that just about anything is right.

Journalist Peggy Orenstein writes that nearly every American now knows a family in which one member came about through in vitro fertilization (IVF) or something like it. She points to the trouble that comes about when, as in our current medical culture, decisions about these things are left solely "to a physician's conscience and a patient's desire." This is compounded, she argues, because "doctors who do IVF are selling a product and their patients are so vulnerable, their experience with infertility so fraught, that they're not always willing or even able to act in what seems like their own best interest." She writes of her own first appointment with a fertility specialist, sitting with her husband, "paging through three-ring binders filled with birth announcements and holiday cards from satisfied customers. How could we help but project ourselves into those albums?"[2]

There are some reproductive technologies that all Christians would agree are ethically acceptable. Like any other medical technology, these treatments seek to correct whatever is malfunctioning in the one-flesh union in order to allow that union to be fruitful. Other technologies, though, step beyond this. They seek to bypass the one-flesh union and so result in children that are, in the words of one Christian ethicist, "made" rather than "begotten." As another Christian ethicist puts it, many of these technologies, such as IVF, result in an objectification of the body and of the child, turning our bodies into instruments rather than creatures.[3] These technologies turn the child into a commodity rather than a gift. This is not simply a Christian concern. Feminists, environmentalists, and even some secular humanists have raised concerns about what the more radical technologies are doing to transform the human experience of procreation.

This is seen even in the way we speak of the whole process, speech that betrays what's going on. Christians thus will ask me often if IVF is okay if they "use all the embryos." They want to assure me that they'll not destroy any of the fertilized eggs (or, as we Christians know them to be, babies) or freeze them in a locker indefinitely. But think about the very way we now speak of these children. They are

---

[2]Peggy Orenstein, "In Vitro We Trust," *New York Times Magazine*, July 20, 2008, 11–12.
[3]Gilbert Meilaender, *Bioethics: A Primer for Christians* (Grand Rapids, MI: Eerdmans, 1996), 11–25.

"used." They are "produced." This is not the pattern of life as a gift given to us by our God.

This ethical morass gets deeper with the kinds of genetic screenings available today. The technology exists—and is getting better—to detect whether or not a fertilized ovum has a predisposition to genetic maladies such as cancer or heart disease. Some even speculate that future screenings will be able to tell parents whether their pre-implanted embryo will be gay. Those who show up with "undesirable" characteristics may be "discarded," and the couple tries again.

The galloping forward of such technologies means we may one day see a world in which only Christians have Down's syndrome babies in their strollers, only Christians have bald little girls fighting through chemotherapy, only Christians have little boys in "husky"-size pants struggling against childhood obesity. What an impoverished world—for all of us—that will be.

How will we talk with our neighbors about the miracle of the new birth when the old one was something they engineered themselves? How will we talk to our neighbors of the unconditional love of a Father for his children, no matter what, when only Christians know what that means?

Other technologies bypass not only the one-flesh nature of the sexual union but the nature of marriage itself. Donor insemination, for instance, and surrogate motherhood bring a third party into the conception of the child. Unlike adoption, wherein the third party already exists, these means intentionally set out to create such a situation. Moreover, unlike adoption, in which both adopting parents participate in the process of adoption, these technologies create a form of techno-step-parenting in which one partner has genetic ties to the child and one does not. Moreover, there is the matter of the commoditization not only of children but also of men and women through this process. Men are not fathers but "sperm donors." Women are not mothers but are harvested for their eggs. Socialist feminist Katha Pollitt rightly points out the exploitation of working-class women, those most likely to be economically desperate enough to rent out their wombs. Pollitt calls the Brave New World of surrogacy "Reproductive Reaganomics."[4] Whatever your opinion of Ronald Reagan's economic program, you know what she means, in the shorthand that leftist columnists use, and you know it's not good.

Unfortunately, too often these ethical questions are simply never explored or addressed, especially by evangelical Christians like me. Just as we lagged behind our Roman Catholic friends on the abortion issue, we seem now to lag behind them on the multitude of new biomedical questions arising all the time. Many of us seem to have a "no abortion, no problem" template through which we evaluate such things—that is, as long as a baby doesn't die and there's no explicit Bible verse to condemn the practice, then it's fine. But there's a larger web of issues here. We rarely ask what we're doing to the cosmic mystery of the marriage union, to our understanding of our bodies and of each other. We rarely ask the question—again in the words of Wendell Berry—"What are people for?"[5]

Even if we completely set aside all ethical concerns, the drive toward extensive reproductive technology still carries a significant moral component, and that is stewardship. Every one of us is accountable for the money God has given us, and all of it is limited, regardless of how wealthy we may believe ourselves to be. Ask yourself—again, prayerfully and with counsel—whether whatever reproductive technology you're using is worth the cost, when those funds could be used to adopt. Think also about the time involved— time that could be spent beginning the process toward becoming a parent. Again, some technologies are worth the time and cost—you can make that case. Sometimes, though, the technologies are inhibiting rather than furthering your quest to be a mom or dad.

So, if you're infertile but reluctant to adopt, what should you do?

First, recognize that this doesn't make you a horrible person, and

---

[4]Liza Mundy, *Everything Conceivable: How Assisted Reproduction Is Changing Men, Women, and the World* (New York: Knopf, 2007), 131.
[5]Wendell Berry, *What Are People For?* (New York: Farrar, Straus, and Giroux, 1990).

it doesn't mean you're not going to adopt eventually. If you're a follower of Jesus, you know the human heart is an awfully complicated set of emotions and motivations. You also know who is Lord over it. Pray and ask the Father to show you whether you should adopt. Ask him, if it's his will for you to be a mother or father through adoption, to give you a desire for it. Ask God to expose any sin or weakness in your life that could hold you back from adopting. Ask him for wisdom in making this decision. He'll do it.

Don't do this alone. Ask your close friends—and older saints in the faith—to join with you in praying for God's will in all this. Freely confess to them your confusion and ambiguity about adoption and request they pray with you that if God wants you to adopt, you'd sense a growing desire to do so. Call the pastors of your church to come to your home and anoint you with oil, praying for God to free you from infertility by granting you children (James 5:13–18). Ask your pastors to pray for God to do this for you either through childbirth or through adoption and if it's adoption to make you, as the psalmist put it, willing in the day of his power (Ps. 110:3). If you do this, don't be surprised if God doesn't start drawing out of you a growing excitement at the prospect of adopting a child (or children). And as he does so, don't be scared by it. It probably means he is pulling you toward your new family, getting you ready for it.

Also, be assured that if the Lord should direct you to adoption, it won't in any sense feel like some sort of consolation prize. Your affection for your child and the permanence of your relationship will be as real to you as if you'd birthed him or her yourself. I know you can't imagine that now, but it's true.

Maybe you're already enthusiastic about the prospect of adoption, but your spouse isn't. That was the case for us. I'm ashamed to say that my wife was checking out adoption options long before I ever wanted to hear about it. Again, cry out to your Father in prayer. Do not subvert your marriage or your sanctification for the sake of the adoption. Husbands, love your wives "as Christ loved the church and gave himself up for her" (Eph. 5:25). This involves leading and teaching, to be sure. Talk with your wife about why you think God's calling you to adoption, but know when to stop talking. Love your wife by, when necessary, bearing with her "as the weaker vessel" (1 Pet. 3:7) as she grieves over losing the experience of bearing a child in her body. Pray for God to redirect that natural longing toward adoption.

Wives, be submissive to your husbands in everything "as to the Lord" (Eph. 5:22). Again, tell your husband what you think the Lord is doing in your life in creating a desire to adopt. But don't prod him. Just as the apostle counsels wives with unbelieving husbands, win him with your life, not with the power of arguments (1 Pet. 3:1–2). Pray for the Lord to bring a unified vision in your home. God loves to do this.

I knew the Lord was calling me to adopt children when suddenly it just seemed right. I'm not a hyper-mystical man, but I do believe that God often shapes our intuitions and impressions in ways we can't explain. When I found myself fantasizing about adopting a baby, the way I'd fantasized about bringing home my son or daughter from the hospital, it was a very rapid shot to my full-on enthusiasm about the whole thing. If God is granting you the desire to adopt children, you should seriously inquire as to whether he's up to something in that arena in your life.

The desire doesn't mean the decision is made. Wisdom is necessary, and as in all things, "Plans are established by counsel; by wise guidance wage war" (Prov. 20:18). Ask godly men and women who know you best whether they think you are morally, psychologically, and financially fit to be parents. Perhaps have a dinner party and gather everyone for a time of prayer and conversation afterward. If your church is equipped for such a thing, ask for a time of congregational prayer and inquire of your fellow members as to their thoughts on the wisdom of your being parents.

Some factors, providentially, would rule out your seeking to adopt. You want your child to have a stable family with two parents (a mother and a father). If you're terminally ill or unemployed, seek to overcome these obstacles (and, yes, I believe in healing; terminal illness may be overcome, should the Lord so desire). Generally speaking, if you're single, pray for a marriage before you seek children. Your marriage might not be everything you ever hoped and dreamed, but don't even consider adoption if either of you are harboring any thoughts of divorce, even if only as a nuclear option in a worst-case scenario. Your children need parents. Don't leave open the possibility that they may be orphans again.

If you're thinking about adoption as a way of bargaining with God, as though he'll repay you for your adoption with "kids of my own" later, then put adoption aside. Your potential children need parents—not to be a pawn in someone's attempt to manipulate the Almighty.

If, though, your life has the stability and love for you to be parents, then pray toward that end, and start walking toward the future that could await you.

Sometimes when adoption becomes a priority for infertile couples, they become almost frantic in their pursuit of children to adopt. The "nesting impulse" of a want-to-be mother is redirected toward paperwork and seminars and so forth. When I first became excited about the prospect of adoption, I wanted to move toward becoming a father by any (legitimate) means necessary. I had a "let a thousand flowers bloom" approach and wanted to cultivate every possibility open to us. Our doctor had suggested a new series of infertility treatments, one that didn't compromise our ethical convictions. I wanted to pursue the medical treatments and pregnancy and the adoption process at the same time. I'll never forget my wife breaking down in my office as she told me she could do one or the other, but she just couldn't do both. She was right.

I am not counseling couples to try to avoid pregnancy during the adoption process, but I would counsel against pursuing extensive fertility treatments and the adoption process simultaneously. A lot of emotional energy is placed in each one of these endeavors, and the simultaneity of it all can leave many potential parents—especially prospective mothers, who bear most of the weight of this—exhausted and discouraged.

If you're not infertile yourself, but you know someone who is, it can be difficult to know exactly how to help, especially when it comes to adoption. Should you suggest that your friends adopt? Should you offer to help them financially or emotionally or by praying for a child for them to adopt?

Some who have spent much time counseling infertile couples would counsel you never to suggest adoption. They argue that this minimizes the grief being suffered by the infertile person or couple and can sound like a simplistic solution. I disagree.

Let me qualify, though, that this depends on *how* you suggest adoption. The situation here is roughly equivalent to the use of Romans 8:28: "And we know that for those who love God all things work together for good, for those who are called according to his purpose." Sometimes people will tell you never to reference this passage to someone who's suffering because it trivializes their suffering. God tells us, though, that "all Scripture" is "profitable for teaching, for reproof, for correction, and for training in righteousness" (2 Tim. 3:16). This passage, and others like it, were given to us for a reason, and part of that reason is for believers to encourage one another with the promises of our God.

There's a way to quote Romans 8:28 as a promise, a promise that groans along with you in the pain involved. There's also a way to quote Romans 8:28 as a dismissal, a way of saying, "Get over it." The first is of the Spirit, the second of the flesh.

The infertility and the miscarriages were difficult for my wife, but they were difficult for me in a completely different way. I know she's a sinner, so I'm sure she sinned through the process—as we all do in every situation—but her response to it all was a sadness. I never saw bitterness spring forth from her. I marveled at seeing her give a baby shower for a friend who had become pregnant at the same time she did—after our baby had died in the womb months earlier—and when the friend's baby was born, Maria was right there in the hospital cooing at the newborn boy. I couldn't help but notice that what had been our baby's due date was only days away.

While my wife experienced sadness, I toyed with, and eventually gave in to, bitterness—a deep and hidden raised fist in the face of God. Once when I left our apartment after one of the miscarriages, so I could get a prescription for Maria, I started the car only to hear on the radio the news that a scandalously immoral, unmarried female celebrity was pregnant—again. I scrunched up my face and breathed out a scoffing "prayer": "How's that just? This woman is pregnant while my sweet and godly wife, who would be an excellent mother, lies sobbing into her pillow upstairs." I think that moment was perhaps the worst sin I've ever committed. I knew far better, but I was calling into question the goodness of my God to me.

That night one of my professors came by our apartment with his wife to see us. I loved this man and respected him because years before I ever knew him, it was his books that convinced me of the inerrancy of Holy Scripture and of the sovereignty of God in all things. He had to teach me those things again that night, without his ever even knowing what he was doing. He and his wife prayed with us, cried with us, expressed their sorrow with us. As he was leaving, he turned in the doorway and just looked at me. Then, after a long pause, he said, "Russell, this thing is terrible. I don't know why it's happening to y'all. But I know God is good. And I know that God will do whatever it takes to conform you into the image of Christ." After he left, my knees literally buckled. I felt what seemed to be literal tremors of conviction come over me as I cried out for mercy from my God.

This friend's words weren't a pat recitation. They were similar to the actions of Jesus at the tomb of Lazarus. Jesus cries out in grief over this death. He has compassion on those left behind. But he also points them to the glorious triumph of God in resurrection power (John 11:1–44).

I would never counsel you to walk up to a couple you don't know but have heard may be infertile and encourage them to adopt. Nor would I ever advise you to suggest adoption with a virtual shrug of your shoulder, as though this would render the infertility no crisis at all. But there's nothing wrong—and much right—with your saying to a friend who longs for children that you'll pray with him or her for God to grant children, through birth or through adoption. And there's nothing wrong—and much right—with suggesting to a couple grieving through infertility that perhaps they should explore whether God is calling them to adoption.

CONSIDERING ADOPTION FOR THOSE WITH ALREADY EXISTING FAMILIES

A few years after we adopted Benjamin and Timothy, the infertility that had plagued Maria and me for years was suddenly lifted, and we gave birth to a son, and then another, in the more typical way. And it was time for the "Are they brothers?" business again, this time from an elderly lady who approached Maria and said, in the hearing of my sons, "I'll bet Dr. Moore is really proud of Samuel." Maria replied, "Yes, he is proud of all of his sons." The lady smiled and retorted, "Yes, but I'll bet he's especially proud of Samuel, since he's his."

In this woman's mind, there was something admirable about adoption, but something especially joyous about a biological son. The sentiment she expressed seemed also to be behind the kind of excited glee some folks had when they first heard Maria was pregnant. "That always happens!" they'd laugh. "Once you adopt, then you get pregnant. Why, my niece . . ." This kind of talk tends to frustrate previously infertile couples because it kind of carries along the myth that infertility goes away when one "relaxes." More than that, though, it seemed to categorize our children into two camps— the "adopted" ones and the "biological" ones. We just didn't (and don't) think that way.

It's not just people who "don't get it," though, who tend to divide kids into these categories. We were surprised to see a friend who had adopted two children shake her head in sadness when she heard about a family with children who were adopting. "It just isn't right," she said. "You should do one or the other, but not both." When we asked why, she told us she thought there was no way one could avoid favoring the biological children. It would be unfair, she thought, to the "adopted" ones. I disagreed at the time, and now after having both "kinds" of children, I disagree even more.

It might be that you have children—biologically—but wonder if the Lord is calling you to adopt. This section of this chapter is much shorter because in some ways your situation is easier than that of an infertile couple. The emotions are not usually so raw. Your situation seems less desperate to you, probably, and so the waiting time is less nerve-wracking. You are pondering whether or not to adopt, but you already know what it is to be a mother or a father.

In some ways, though, your decision may be even more complex. Your friends and family members may be perplexed as to why you would adopt. "Don't you have your own kids?" they may ask. You may wonder if a family with both "biological" and "non-biological" children will be unfair to either set. And you may wonder whether you are selfish for "getting" a child who could be adopted by a couple without children.

I've often wondered about the censure our friend had for the family with "both kinds" of children, "biological" and "adopted," about whether she realized her attitudes were built off the same foundation as those who would dismiss her family as not being "real." Both assume a fundamental division between parents based on biology and parents based on adoption. Rebecca Walker, author of a popular memoir on becoming a mother, sums up this attitude. Walker, who was a mother figure for her former lover's child, argues that being an "adoptive parent" involves "a lesser kind of love than the love for a biological child." I found Walker's rationale to be revealing. She says that for her, it all comes down to the fact that she'd die for her biological child, but she was "not sure I would do that for my non-biological child." Walker concedes in an interview,

"I mean, it's an awful thing to say. The good thing is he has a biological mom who would die for him."[6]

This makes sense only for someone who's never seen adopting love that is willing to die. You have. As we discussed earlier, your adoption in Christ came through a Father willing to sacrifice his only begotten Son, an older brother willing to bear the weight of the sins of the world, to bring you into the household. And once you arrived, you found you have the exact same standing as the children who were already there (Eph. 2:19). There is no reason why, through the Spirit, you would love or favor your children "according to the flesh" any differently than you love the children you've adopted.

That's not to say there's not a certain amount of common sense—and plain honesty—in what Walker and others like her are saying. A woman once wrote me, a stepmother who was having terrible difficulty building a relationship with her stepchild, about this very issue. She remarked about the "tenacity of what I'll call 'blood-tiedness,'" a tenacity she could hardly overcome. "Consider our innate blindness to the flaws of our children or grandchildren that we don't have to the flaws of someone else's," she wrote. "We are also uniquely embarrassed by family members. When holidays arrive, or at the end of our lives, something inexorably tugs us back to our families." This woman pointed out that the "dividing wall" of Ephesians 2:14 demonstrates something of this. "It's not a weak wall," she wrote. "It's just that he's an immensely powerful God."

That's precisely the point. You are indeed designed to love "your own flesh and blood," but your design is redeemed in Christ to see as your flesh and blood those whom you previously didn't recognize as such.

This frustrated stepmother pointed to the example of Moses as evidence that biology trumps adoption in terms of familial affection and personal identity. Moses, you'll remember, escapes Pharaoh's decree to kill the Hebrew children because his mother hides him in

---

[6]Stephanie Rosenbloom, "Evolution of a Feminist Daughter," *New York Times*, March 18, 2007, 9.12.

a basket in the river. When Pharaoh's daughter is bathing, she finds the basket, and the baby. Pharaoh's daughter immediately recognizes the lad as "one of the Hebrews' children," and Moses' sister is there to suggest a Hebrew nursemaid for the child. Moses is nursed and raised by his very own birth mother. It is not until he "grew up" that he comes into Pharaoh's court and is pronounced the son of Pharaoh's daughter (Ex. 2:1–10).

Moses is eventually coercively separated from his birth family, but he retains his Jewish identity from birth. He grows up among his flesh-and-blood kin, nurtured in his mother's lap. This is hardly the kind of permanent adopting situation seen in God's adoption of us in Christ. That is found in Joseph's adoption of Jesus and Naomi's adoption of Ruth, but not in Moses' adoption by Pharaoh's family.

Yes, there will be some who don't understand why you'd want to adopt. Some of them may even be related to you. This is because for many who've never experienced adoption, adoption seems to be simply a Plan B for people who can't have children. They're not able to see the beauty of adoption in and of itself. So be it. What better opportunity for you to model the God who adopts from every tongue, tribe, nation, and language and sets all the children together at the same table with the same inheritance and the same love? When you get puzzled looks from people who don't understand, just smile and tell them how happy you are for God's kindness to you, that you're grateful that he's blessing you again.

There is no reason whatsoever for you to feel guilty, as though you are "taking scarce resources" by adopting a child when there are childless couples out there seeking to adopt. First of all, a child isn't a "resource." He or she is a human being, created in the image of God. Secondly, there are more children needing homes than loving Christian parents who are willing to take them in. You are not taking a child away from another prospective adoptive family. To the contrary, if the Lord does lead you to a child through adoption, this adoption could very well be a catalyst to create a more adoption-friendly environment in your church and neighborhood. The very presence of your children on the playground or in the Sunday school class could make adoption less "strange" to the people around you. That can only help parentless children and childless parents find one another through adoption as churches and families cooperate in the task.

If you already have children, your situation is made more complicated by the fact that you have the responsibility not simply for your spouse and your prospective child but for the children God has already given you. This means you'll need to think through how an adoption would affect your already existing family. Now, I am not suggesting this means taking a poll, any more than you would simply gauge your children's interest in whether or not they'd like to have vaccinations this year. You are responsible before God for determining with wisdom what's best for your children. You certainly will talk with your children and weigh their reaction to the possibility of a new brother or sister, but the decision runs deeper than this.

Some children would react negatively if they heard Mom was pregnant, and some children would celebrate Mom's pregnancy— without knowing about the severe diabetes that makes the pregnancy life-threatening. In the same way, sometimes children who initially resent a new adopted child find their initial reluctance vaporizing as they grow to love their new brother or sister. And sometimes children who love the idea of a new sibling find the reality less idyllic than they thought when it actually happens.

If the Spirit is drawing you toward adopting, think of the opportunity you'll have to share the gospel with your already-here children. Think of how you'll be able to involve them in the process—collecting money from odd jobs for the adoption fees, painting the nursery or new bedroom, praying each night for the new brother or sister. They'll see before their very eyes the kind of welcoming gospel you pray they—and their children and grandchildren—will embrace. Perhaps God has blessed you financially, and he's calling you to show your children that a Christian family will give account for these funds one day. Maybe he's calling you to show them that money invested in the life of a son or daughter is wiser than money invested in a boat or a motorcycle or a summer cruise.

One issue that arises for those with children as they seek to discern whether adoption is for them is the question of birth order. Much has been written and lectured about birth order in recent years, and some of it is pop psychology nonsense. Your birth order doesn't fatalistically map out who you're going to be or how you're going to behave. There are plenty of passive firstborns out there, and we've all known the baby of the family who's chairman of the board. That said, birth order is clearly not irrelevant either.

God designed us so that we learn who we are and what we're about partly through how we fit into our household economy. The sudden change of a firstborn to a second child can be a traumatic experience. Generally speaking, I would seek to adopt children younger than my oldest child, especially if they're of the same sex. There are, of course, going to be exceptions to this that are providentially arranged, but the place the existing children have in the family should be taken into consideration.

You'll want to ask whether you're able to carry out your responsibilities to your current children and to the potential new children. Fathers, are you able to provide financially for your children? Let me explain that you do not need lots of money. God never commands fathers to provide designer clothing and electronic gadgets and trips to theme parks for their children. Are you able to feed, clothe, and shelter your children? Are you able to keep them from the peril of homelessness or dislocation or public assistance? Mothers, are you able to nurture your children, even with a new son or daughter in the home?

Again, I am not referring to the contemporary myth that parental attention weakens with the addition of every child. Most families in the history of the world have been larger than contemporary Western expectations. Large families are often as loving and affectionate—or more so—than small families where one might assume each child has more of a shot at one-on-one attention.

Moreover, the feeling of stress with your current children needn't put an end to the possibility that you could adopt. Every parent feels stressed—and sometimes overwhelmed. The question is not whether you sometimes feel overwhelmed but whether you are, in fact, overwhelmed by your responsibilities as parents. If you're harsh or neglectful or resentful of your current children, if you won't discipline or won't show affection, repent of these things before you start the adoption process. A new child won't create you, *ex nihilo*, into a godly parent.

Just as with an infertile couple, you should seek counsel. If you're in a situation where your pastors know you well enough (and I hope you are), ask them if they believe you should adopt. If they have concerns related to your current children, seek to discern where you're having difficulty being godly parents and seek sanctification in those things before you pursue adoption. Invite wise, discerning, spiritual friends over to counsel with you about whether God has given you the ability to be parents to more children than those he's already given you.

Sometimes God will spring adoption on you unexpectedly. A family member may die, leaving behind children. You may get a call in the night from a friend who knows a teenage girl who's contemplating abortion but would give the baby up to a couple she can trust. Some friends of ours, with five children in their home, received word one day that a mother in their community wanted to give up the daughter she'd adopted years earlier. Our friends intervened to keep this beautiful little one from being sent into the state foster care system, and they were parents again within the week.

As with couples without children, the issue for you involves desire, wisdom, and providence. If the Lord grants you a longing to adopt a child or children, if wise discernment and outside counsel determine your fitness for it, and if the circumstances God arranges in your life put adoption in your story, then God probably is calling you to adopt. If so, gather your children around, and let them share in the joy of what God is doing in your family. He's allowing you to join him in his plan for yet another child to grow up hearing the story of Christ, with a family that names the name of Jesus. God's fitting you into his purpose, "that a people yet to be created may praise the LORD" (Ps. 102:18).

CONCLUSION

At one level, the question that frames this chapter is easily answered, indeed has already been answered. The Father adopts children, and we're called to be like him. Jesus cares for orphans, and we're being conformed into his image. If you're in Christ, you're called to be involved in this project somehow. That doesn't mean, though, that your family, personally, is equipped to adopt a child right now. I suspect, though, that there are far more people out there, maybe you, who could adopt but who simply haven't thought about it. What would it hurt to ask the Spirit to show you if you're to image God through adoption?

In this sense, the priority of adoption is kind of like global missions. Missionaries often say—and rightly, I believe—that the question one should ask is not whether he is called to missions but how. One shouldn't ask first, "Am I called to take the gospel to the nations?" but "Am I called to support the Great Commission from home?" A similar principle is at work here. Some people "feel called" to the mission field but clearly shouldn't go. Many more should be there—or should be funneling prayer support and monetary aid to those preaching overseas—who haven't even considered how they fit into God's global purposes. Some of you may feel called to adopt children, but you clearly shouldn't. Maybe your marriage is in trouble, or you lack self-control in your finances or your anger or your work ethic. Probably many more of you would make excellent parents—for the first time or again—if you'd just make yourself vulnerable enough before your God to ask.

Most significantly, the decision-making process about adoption has to recognize the goodness of God's purposes, both over the universe in general and over your life in particular. The Bible tells us that God is writing a big story, a story centered on Jesus. If you're in Christ, God is at work directing your little story to fit into the plot of the big story. Your situation, whether with an empty cradle or a kitchen floor full of babies, may well play into that. God may be preparing you to be the kind of people who can better display Christ to a new generation.

I never thought I'd struggle with infertility or miscarriages. It literally never occurred to me at all. As a matter of fact, when I married, my attitude was one of fear of children. I wanted children, to be sure, but I wanted to make sure they arrived later, when we could "afford" them and when they could fit into our life plan. That seemed to be the reasonable, common-sense attitude to have. All the baby-boomer adults in my life, including in my church, had warned us, after all, when we married, "Be sure you don't have kids too early. Have time to enjoy each other." So my honeymoon plans included me nervously packing multiple forms of contraception. All along I looked forward to being a dad, when I was ready to be one. I suppose I thought I'd look at a financial statement, make the call, come home and, well, start the project, and the baby would arrive right on time, forty weeks later.

The infertility and the miscarriages shook me from that self-sufficiency (at least in that area; there's a long way to go in many others). Having children easily would have been dangerous for me. I'd have seen my children as "offspring" in the most literal sense of that word—those expected things that spring off my life as planned. The prospect of not having children was dangerous for me too. It offered the temptation, old as the first garden, to wonder whether my wisdom and my power were better than Christ, the Wisdom and Power of God.

Some of you may be in either of those predicaments right now, and perhaps you're learning why the book of Proverbs includes the prayer, "Give me neither poverty nor riches; feed me with the food that is needful for me, lest I be full and deny you and say, 'Who is the LORD?' or lest I be poor and steal and profane the name of my God" (30:8–9). Perhaps you're learning to live out what Paul writes: "I know how to be brought low, and I know how to abound. In any and every circumstance, I have learned the secret of facing plenty and hunger, abundance and need. I can do all things through him who strengthens me" (Phil. 4:12–13).

Infertility isn't good. Miscarriages are evil. Death is horrible. I don't shrug my shoulders in resignation at those things. I lost three children, children I'll never know until resurrection morning. But even in this, God was working all things together for good. God's purpose was good in the big, cosmic sense, of course; he's moving history along to the reign of Christ. But it was good for me personally too, even just in the course of this little life. If it hadn't been for the infertility, for the miscarriages, my wife and I never would have traveled across the ocean to that orphanage. We would have children in the Christmas card photographs, but they wouldn't include Benjamin and Timothy. Our lives would have been impoverished, and we wouldn't even have known it.

I can't tell you whether or not God's calling you, personally, to adopt a child. I can tell you he has a plan for you, a plan that includes picturing his adopting grace and his protection of the fatherless. I can also tell you he's good to you, even when—maybe especially when—he's up to things you can't understand. Maybe he's leading you to the joy of adoption, taking you the long way around.

God often doesn't explain his providence to us, past or future. He asks us to trust him, to endure, and to know, in the words of the old gospel song, that we'll "understand it better by and by." Sometimes, though, he grants us a glimpse in the middle of it all of how he's silently working toward something joyous.

The other day I was driving around the city, running errands with my boys, while Maria was at a women's event with our church. I had the music playing in the car, set to a random selection of my list of songs. My older boys had sung along with Waylon Jennings and Willie Nelson singing about Luckenbach, Texas. We heard the familiar strands of Michael Card's brilliant lyrics on the way of wisdom. We even enjoyed a Christian hip-hop artist rapping about the Trinity and the hypostatic union.

Then the random selection of music hit upon a 1990s Christian song I hadn't heard in a long, long time. It was Wes King's "Thought You'd Be Here." I stopped singing along, and the car grew quiet as I listened to those words I'd heard so many times just a few years ago. My sons probably wondered why I was wiping away tears, looking at my steering wheel.

Then the lyrics turned to that line, the line that used to evoke such hollowness in me: "I never knew the silence could make me so deaf / I never knew that I could miss someone I'd never met, miss someone I hadn't met . . . yet." Just then, I looked into the backseat via the rear-view mirror. I saw four little faces looking back at me. And the littlest face was topped off with a blue denim cap.

5

Paperwork, Finances, and Other Threats to Personal Sanctification

How to Navigate the Practical Aspects of the Adoption Process

IN MY FAMILY LINE, we've had televangelist-watching Roman Catholics and alcoholic Southern Baptists, right-wing Democrats and welfare-state Republicans, and every other possible belief system in between all of those. One thing, though, that my family has seemed to have unanimity on as far as anyone can remember is that we just do not believe in cats in the house. A table full of fighting Moores will gain instant consensus if someone ever raises the possibility of such a thing. I'm no exception to this conviction—blame it on nature, nurture, or (if you agree with me) on just good old common sense.

I'll make an exception, gladly, though for an outside cat, especially if there's a mouse problem afoot. That was our situation about a year after the boys arrived in our home. The garage outside would have birdseed strewn across the floor from another punctured bag. The umbrella strollers we had propped against the wall would be littered with droppings. And the mousetraps I'd set would have the peanut butter eaten from them, with nary a mouse corpse in sight. It was time for a tomcat to put an end to all this.

Maria placed a call to the animal protection agency here in our city to see if we could go pick out a cat from the pound. The official on the other end of the phone said they'd have to send someone out to do a "home study" to see if our house was fit for a cat. Maria explained that the cat would be outside, though it would sleep in the garage when it was cold. The animal protection lady gasped in shock, as though Maria had told her we planned to serve boiled bulldog at our next dinner party. "Oh, ma'am!" the woman exclaimed. "We would never allow one of our cats to be placed in a home that would put him or her outside." When I arrived home that evening, Maria informed me we were qualified by the Commonwealth of Kentucky to be fit to have two children but not one cat.

That entire ridiculous situation reminded both of us that the adoption process hadn't been as difficult—or as much of a clash of worldviews—as we'd expected. In fact, it seemed at the time to be much more problematic than it was, simply because we were always holding our breath for whatever was coming next (and we knew it would be something bad).

Adoption, as I've mentioned, is spiritual warfare in the heavenly places. But on the earthly plane it's probably easier than you think. It's war, but it's not hell. If you or someone you love is considering adoption, there are lots of decisions to be made and paperwork to be completed. Of course, much of this will differ from state to state and region to region, and certainly from nation to nation.

The following suggestions are just that, suggestions for Christians moving toward parenthood through adoption. As in everything else about our sanctification, the true tests are rarely as spectacular as we expect they'd be. The same is true here. The glory of adoption has to do with some seemingly small decisions and some frustrating and mundane tasks—like paperwork, home studies, and waiting.

BASIC DECISIONS

Sometimes when I'm counseling couples seeking adoption, they ask why we chose to adopt internationally and why we chose Russia. It would sound good to say we've had a lifelong burden for the former Soviet Union, that God laid the Rostov region of Russia on our hearts, or that we had some religious liberty issue that kept us, by conviction, from adopting domestically. But none of that's true. It's just how things turned out.

At that moment in history, adopting from Russia was the fastest, least bureaucratically burdensome option we could find. Plus, the agency we found had experience and expertise with Russian adoption. That's it. God was up to more than this, of course, but we didn't know it at the time.

Many of you will find the same thing's true for you. The decisions you make aren't large-scale philosophical decisions; they're just what seem best at the time. As you think about adoption, though, there will be some preliminary, foundational decisions you'll have to make, decisions that will set the course of the rest of the process.

Domestic or International Adoption

Domestic adoption—that is, adopting from somewhere within your own country—carries with it extraordinary missional possibilities. After all, there are children in this country who need to be adopted, many of them languishing in foster care systems and many of them with special needs. For some of you, domestic adoption might not be a decision you make, necessarily, but just something that seems to happen. For instance, a family member might die or abandon his or her family, leaving you with custody of his or her children, and this may lead to your adopting these children. Perhaps you've married a widow or widower or divorcee and are contemplating adopting his or her child as your own. It may be that you're aware of a pregnant woman in a crisis situation—usually a single woman—who is thinking about making an adoption plan for her baby. I've known several couples who have received calls, unexpectedly, from pastors or friends saying, "I'm talking to a pregnant young lady, trying to talk her out of abortion. If she agrees to the adoption, would you take the baby?" These serendipitous kinds of adoption sometimes happen without an agency, through a private process with an attorney. If so, you'll want to find an attorney who has expertise in adoption.

Domestic adoptions can also happen through an adoption

agency, perhaps even through a Christian children's home in your area. If so, you can make application through the agency and wait for the agency to put you in touch with a child or, in some cases, with a birth mother. Often domestic adoptions happen via the foster care system. In a foster adoption, the children live, for a time, in a kind of halfway point, somewhere short of adoption, with a family. Sometimes a child moves from foster family to foster family in succession before being adopted. Many Christian families seek to bring the presence of Christ's kingdom to the foster care system by signing up as foster parents. Some of these families don't ever adopt but seek to bring a Christian influence on children for a time, before other families adopt the children.

Domestic adoption carries with it some particular risks, and these risks are dependent to a large degree on the laws of your state or locality. An adoption often carries the possibility that the birth mother will change her mind. Anyone attentive to adoption has known a couple who excitedly worked with a birth mother for months—praying with her, choosing names with her, discussing the future with her—only to have the mother decide, once she had the baby, not to proceed with the adoption. From a Christian view of things, it's easy to see how this could happen. God has designed women to be "mothers" (Gen. 3:20), and no matter what her crisis, when the baby is born it is very, very difficult to sever that natural bond between mother and child. "Can a woman forget her nursing child, that she should have no compassion on the son of her womb?" God asks his people, with the implication that such a suggestion would be absurd. "Even these may forget, yet I will not forget you" (Isa. 49:15). Many birth mothers understand the goodness of adoption in their situation and channel their maternal design into the best interest of the child when that best interest is adoption into a stable, loving family.

Occasionally, though, a birth mother will not see things this way. A birth mother is grieving the loss of a child, but the child is not dead. She's experiencing the "Rachel weeping for her children" type of despair, and sometimes it seems as though keeping the baby is a way to protect the child. This is one reason why having an agency involved can be a good thing. Agency personnel are trained to counsel prospective parents and birth mothers, seeking to help both "sides" reach and keep consensus.

Additionally, most states grant a birth mother a specified length of time to change her mind about the adoption before surrendering her parental rights. This time varies state to state, and in some states it can be relatively lengthy. To adopting parents, this can seem *very* lengthy, especially if the parents have been through a long time of infertility or miscarriage, heightening what already seems to be an anxiety-provoking scenario. One adopting father told me he spent the time during that waiting period waking up repeatedly every night, fearful of hearing a phone call from the birth mother. "I wasn't exactly holed up in a tree stand outside with a shotgun," he said. "But I was almost afraid I would be by the end of it all." That said, the vast, vast majority of domestic adoptions don't include the kind of drama that shows up on the nightly news broadcasts of weeping adoptive parents returning their baby to the birth parents.

After the legal surrender of parental rights, the child is the son or daughter of his or her new parents. In the meantime, the adopting parents usually have a way to avoid the heartache of such risk—waiting to take the baby home only after the birth parents have signed the legal documents surrendering parental rights. Of course, many other adopting parents bring their babies home before this, knowing the risks involved.

Domestic adoption usually brings the additional benefit of greater knowledge about the background of one's child. One is much more likely to know the child's familial medical history and other pertinent information—such as, for instance, whether he's ever been physically or sexually abused—if one adopts domestically.

The foster care system, like the public school system, differs from place to place. In some places, foster care is an effortless way to quickly move toward adoption. Once a family complies with the mandated training and certification, that family can help restore a child to his parents—sometimes parents having difficulty with familial breakdown or substance abuse. In many situations, Christian foster parents have seen birth parents and foster children come to faith in Jesus through the witness of the family.

In some places, it's difficult for Christian families to parent in keeping with their convictions via the foster care system. For one thing, the uncertainty of the situation tends sometimes to force a necessary distance. Neither the parents nor the child know whether the situation is permanent or temporary. The kind of affection, then, necessary for a complete bonding, the "Abba" cry, is held in suspended animation. Similarly, some state laws severely restrict the use of corporal punishment in discipline. It's quite easy to see why the authorities would do this, given the kind of physical abuse some of the children have faced. I actually agree with the policy—not because I oppose corporal punishment but because I think that is exclusively a parental responsibility (Heb. 12:7–8). It can be difficult, though, for Christian families who know the creational good of discipline to resort to time-outs with children when they know a consistently applied, mild spanking would do much more good. It also can be somewhat difficult to make the transition, when the adoption does take place, to a disciplined life in the family. Difficulty does not mean impossibility, though. Even in the most bureaucratically Byzantine and even thoroughly secularist situations, there are Christians bearing witness—like the Christ-followers among the imperial guard in the first century (Phil. 1:13).

A new, and evolving, form of domestic adoption is what's sometimes called embryo adoption or "snowflake adoption." This is the adoption of frozen embryos (I'm using here the current scientific designation for purposes of clarity, not to deny the full personhood of these unborn persons) stored in fertility clinics as the "extras" from in vitro fertilization projects. Some Christian couples sense a particular burden to rescue these tiny brothers and sisters kept now in suspended animation in freezers. This kind of adoption allows the adopting mother to experience pregnancy as she carries the baby or babies in her womb.

Christians often wonder about the ethical justice of "snowflake adoption." Isn't this simply an embrace of the kind of "Brave New World" Frankenstein technology we elsewhere lament? No. First of all, adopting parents are not complicit in the "production" (I shudder to type such a horrible word in reference to a human creature) of these children. The children are already conceived; the adopting parents are no more endorsing the technologies involved than parents adopting from an unwed mother are endorsing fornication. Embryo adoption also doesn't carry with it the violence to the one-flesh union that comes with surrogacy or sperm donation, in which one spouse's genetic material is joined with a stranger's. Embryo adoption would be problematic if the adoptions themselves became a further commodity in the buying and selling transactions of the reproductive technology business or if these adoptions were a widespread incentive for couples to justify the decision to "create" and freeze additional embryos. This is not, though, presently the case and doesn't appear to be likely to become so anytime soon.

International adoption—that is, adopting from a country outside of one's own—has a distinctly Great Commission aspect to it. Many of the cultures from which Christian families may adopt have little or no culture of adoption. Families adopting from China, for instance, will most often be adopting little girls, many of whom are discarded because females are not as valued, especially with the Chinese Communist government's oppressive and coercive population control program. Families adopting from other areas of the world will sometimes be delivering orphans from situations in which their extended families are stricken with AIDS or some other dread disease. Additionally, some of the countries from which families may adopt have little, if any, exposure to the gospel. International adoption can be the means the Spirit uses to proclaim Christ among peoples where Christ is not yet named.

International adoption also is often much quicker and less

bureaucratically entangled than domestic adoption. There is also, in most international adoption situations, immediateness to the creation of the new family. There is, at least in most international situations, little chance of a birth mother or birth father changing her or his mind during or after the adoption process. Indeed, there's little chance that the birth parents will ever show up at one's door five, ten, or thirty years later. The new family is the new family, with very little of an in-between stage.

This is also a negative aspect, though, of many international adoptions. One often has extremely limited information about the personal or familial health history of the children. Our pediatrician would like to know, for instance, if there's any family history of, say, childhood diabetes. I just don't know and never will. Another family told me once of their not being able to determine whether their daughter, adopted from overseas as a toddler, had been abused. They had no information from the orphanage but were concerned about the way she'd flinch whenever a hand came near her face to brush her hair or to pat her cheeks. That information wouldn't have changed whether this family wanted her, but it would make a difference in their extra sensitivity to making her know she is wanted and protected.

Another risk involved in international adoption is that of shady operations in some countries, including baby-selling operations in which impoverished families are coerced, by their desperate circumstances, to give their children up for adoption. International humanitarian organizations and government agencies monitor reports of such activity. The U.S. State Department has shut down adoptions from some areas, due to corruption and coercive adoption. Going through a reputable, licensed agency will avoid putting oneself in this kind of ethically reprehensible situation. As in the case of birth mothers suing adopting parents for custody years later, such situations are much more rare than one might think from watching television news reports. Adoptions—or anything else—that go right are not nearly as newsworthy as those that go wrong.

Of course, there are those who see baby selling in any kind of international adoption, since the women involved often give their children away because of crushing poverty. Some of these critics of international adoption see the practice as "imperialist," with wealthy nations adopting from impoverished nations. Of course, we must remember that this "imperialist" critique also is used against Christian missionary enterprises. Moreover, the ethical objections often are shortsighted, reminding me of the parody sign seen at a protest rally, "Stop Disease; Medicine Is Not the Answer."

Yes, many women in impoverished countries proceed with adoption because of their economic plights. But they are not giving these children away specifically because there are adoptions available. If this were the case, there wouldn't be full orphanages in regions that aren't open for international adoption. In caring for orphans and widows, Christians should work for justice on the international scene at both the *macro* and *micro* levels. We should help in every way open to us to create the kinds of economic and agricultural conditions in which poverty is alleviated. We should also work to help individual children who are sentenced to life as orphans through no fault of their own. The *macro* and *micro* levels of compassion are not in conflict with one another.

With international adoption, there's always the possibility of a country closing itself to international adoptions. This isn't because these countries are evil or anti-child, necessarily. Sometimes it's the reverse. They hear, for instance, of publicized cases where children from their country have been abused, and officials naturally begin to wonder if international adoption is safe for children. Plus there is the matter of how wounding the very idea is to one's concept of national identity. Imagine that the United States had lost the Cold War, and the USA had broken apart into its respective states, each now Communist but impoverished and seemingly unable to cope with the new global Marxist economy. And imagine further that wealthy Soviet government officials were adopting American children from orphanages, taking them back to the USSR to be good

Stalinist comrades for the next generation. There'd be a great deal of humiliation and hostility wrapped up in that. Some countries allow international adoption in spite of popular distaste for it. All kinds of other economic and political factors might cause a given country to pause or shut down adoptions.

Again, having an experienced agency is the key to avoiding such problems. Agencies that maintain their licenses in the relevant countries and have good "intelligence" about the state of adoption law in these countries usually keep families from getting caught in such international trauma. Additionally, most agencies are equipped, if a country does close to adoptions, to move relatively painlessly to another country that's opening up to adoption.

Open or Closed Adoption

The "are they brothers?" question my wife and I often got about our boys rarely stood alone. It was usually coupled with something along the lines of "So have you ever seen their mother?" I would usually respond with a quip. "Sure, and so have you. Have you met Maria?" But I knew what they meant.

Truth is, we weren't told much at all about the boys' birth mothers, beyond their ages and the number of children they were known to have abandoned previously. But there was one picture.

Before the orphanage personnel took us in to see the boys for the first time, they showed us a copy of a passport photograph of the birth mother of one of them. We were told that we couldn't take the picture with us or make a copy or even snap a photo of the photo. We could look at it then and then never see it again. This was the first and last time that we'd ever see the face of the woman who'd given birth to one of our sons.

My first thought was that she looked so young, like one of the gum-popping, hair-twirling girls in the church I'd once served as youth minister. My second thought was that she was beautiful, in an Audrey Hepburn kind of way. Her soft features were nothing like the severe visages of most of the Russian women we'd met so far on this trip. She looked sad to me, but I wondered how much of that had to do with the fact that she was an unwed mother giving away her child and how much had to do with the fact that, well, very few of us look happy in a government-issued identification badge.

As I looked at the picture, a series of questions came to mind about this mysterious young girl. Did she listen to American pop music with her friends, like the girls we'd seen earlier that day in the town square, smoking cigarettes and laughing together as they danced? Had she ever heard the gospel? What did she think of the Jesus pictured all around the village in Orthodox icons on the walls? Did she fall in love with the wrong boy? Did he promise her he'd marry her once he landed a job in the tractor factory in the next town over? Was she married young to a hard-drinking miner who announced he couldn't support another baby? I didn't know, and I never would.

I stared at that passport with more intensity than I've ever looked at anything. It felt like I was given two minutes to look at an answer key before entering a room to take an exam that would determine my entire future. Or, closer to the truth, I felt like a police sketch artist, looking at a suspect's face that I'd have to re-create on paper one day soon. It wasn't idle curiosity.

I was trying to memorize this woman's face for him, for whoever my son would be. I knew once this adoption was completed, the records would be lost to us and to him, probably forever. This tiny, impoverished village wouldn't keep a searchable database of archival materials. If ever my son were to know anything about the woman who gave him life, I'd have to remember for him. Maybe he'd never ask; maybe it would never bother him. But I doubted that. There'd come a day when he'd wonder about her—maybe when he's holding his own baby daughter for the first time, maybe when he's consoling me at the funeral of my mother. He'd want to know about her, and I wanted to be able to describe to him her eyes, the shape of her face, the way her hair hung around her face. If I didn't remember for him, she'd be lost to him.

Sometimes I think about her when I'm watching his face, trying to see whether it looks anything like that passport photo. Did she have that dimple he has in his chin? I wonder if she chattered when she was nervous, as he does now. I wonder if she ever thinks about him, wherever she is. Could she imagine the way he turns and waves to the crowd when he hits a baseball in a Little League game? Could she believe how he memorizes Scripture verses for his Sunday school classes at church? Would she recognize him at all? Would she care?

The image of that passport photo is fading in my memory. I can still see it, but how much of it is her and how much of it is Audrey Hepburn, with my mind playing tricks on me since it made that comparison so early on? I feel like I'm forgetting her, and I can't do that. My memory is the only link my son has to his past. My son may never know anything more about his birth mother than what I can describe from that remembered photo, along with my gratitude to this mysterious woman for giving life to my sweet little man. That's a weighty burden for me as a father, and it will be a unique burden for my son, perhaps, one day.

In our case, there was no decision made about how involved the birth mothers would be in our lives or in the lives of our boys. Even if we had wanted an open, cooperative adoption, we couldn't have done it with our boys. The birth mothers were out of sight and impossible to track down. In like manner, for many of you there will be no choice about whether the adoption is open or closed. Some of you will have situations similar to ours, where there is almost no trace of the original family. Some of you will make adoption plans with birth mothers who want to negotiate some form of open adoption, and you'll have little choice in the matter. For the rest of you, though, the choice of an open or closed adoption will be a decision you'll need to think through.

The decision about whether you'll want to pursue an open or closed adoption is essentially a choice about how involved you'll want the birth mother (or birth father—rarely the case, sadly) to be in the life of your child and family after the adoption. In an open adoption the birth parents retain some contact. This could range from a yearly Christmas letter to weekend visits. In closed adoptions the adopting family becomes the new family, with little or no contact retained with the birth family. Sometimes closed adoptions—especially in international adoptions—means virtually no information about the birth family. Open adoptions are far more common than in years past and are becoming more common. Birth mothers sometimes, at least at first, want to retain the option of seeing their baby as he or she grows up.

For Christians, the questions about open and closed adoption have special significance, because we believe we're not constructing the adoption process as we go but are instead copying a preexisting spiritual reality.

Obviously, the secrecy and shame related to closed adoptions in generations past aren't fitting for a Christian ethic, but such aspects are almost never the case today. A relatively open adoption might be the best option for you. It could be entirely appropriate for you to keep in touch with a birth mother or grandparents via cards, letters, and photographs as the child grows up, when this is possible. Such contact honors the birth mother—an honor that is due, especially, in an age when she could easily have aborted the child—and adopting parents have nothing to fear from giving such honor where it is due.

Additionally, many adoptions now don't fit very neatly into the open or closed categories. Some families opt to send pictures and information about the child to the birth parents through their agency. In this way, a birth mother or birth father can see the life and progress of the child without being directly involved in his or her life. The flow of information is one way. In this scenario, the family sends along letters or photographs to the agency, which then forwards these things to the birth parents, with no direct contact made. In this case, the birth parent doesn't even know, perhaps, the last name, address, or telephone number of the new family. Other families opt for a semi-open arrangement in which the adopting family maintains limited contact with the birth parent, perhaps through an e-mail account without specific identifying information (last names, telephone numbers, etc.).[1]

A friend of ours adopted a child when another family, who had adopted her internationally, severed parental rights and gave her up for adoption. The mother was the one driving the decision to give the child up, while the father appeared passive and guilt-stricken. Occasionally he'll send along a card with some money to his former child at her new parents' address. This doesn't cause a problem for this family, precisely because there's no confusion in the child's understanding about who Mommy and Daddy are.

At the same time, though, many open adoptions are so open as to rob children of the safety and security of a family. Adoption isn't shared custody. Adoption creates a new family. A family has a definition, embedded in the biblical revelation and in the natural order. An adoption that leaves a child with "two mommies" or confused paternity isn't in the best interest of the child.

A family told me not long ago about their mixed experience with open adoption. In the case of their first child, the openness of the adoption was a blessing rather than a burden. They send pictures several times a year to the birth mother and to the birth grandmother. In the case of their second child, however, they find themselves with an ongoing contact with a birth mother who wants not only contact with their child but also to be "part of the family." This is confusing for the child, as you can imagine. It's also put strain on the family in ways they never imagined. The birth mother weighed in, for instance, about a possible move necessitated by the father's transfer at work. If you elect for open adoption, the terms of expectations of both sides should be clear from the beginning. You also should think through with wisdom and discernment whether the adoption is so open that it is an obstacle to your child's full envelopment into your family and its story.

---

[1] I am indebted to my friend Justin Taylor for ideas on semi-open adoption strategies. He shared these with me via e-mail as we conversed about various issues related to our common adoption stories.

Our adoption in Christ means a transfer from an old fatherhood to a new one. We are no longer Satan's children, though he disputes the custody arrangement—and we feel pulled in the meantime—right up until our final adoption at the resurrection from the dead. This doesn't mean that birth parents are to be equated with Satan—not at all. It does mean, though, that adoption forms and creates a new reality, a new family. Whether an adoption is open or closed, adopting parents should be sure, from the beginning, not to surrender parental identity or authority. You may decide it's in your child's best interest to retain some contact with a birth relative, but make sure you retain sole responsibility as mother and father.

PAPERWORK AND HOME STUDIES

If the Lord is calling you to adopt, he's calling you to sign your name . . . over and over and over again. In almost any adoption, there's a pile of paperwork to be completed, regulations to be adhered to, protocols to be acknowledged. Again, this is not as daunting as it first appears.

For some adopting parents, no agency is needed. They know of a child who needs to be adopted—perhaps they are aware of an expectant birth mother; so an adoption attorney is contacted, and the process is made legal. In most situations, though, whether domestic or international, prospective parents will need an agency. Agency workers serve as guides. They've been through the process multiple times, so they know how to navigate the system. They also are less emotionally invested than the prospective parents, so they're not going to be overwhelmed by the foreignness of the process. In a domestic adoption, an agency is invaluable in providing the necessary counseling with the birth mother and setting the terms of the adoption, right up to the best way for the birth mother to say good-bye to her baby and hand him over to his new parents. In an international adoption, an agency is crucial in equipping families to meet the (sometimes contradictory) legal requirements of the different state and national governments involved. One's agency will set up transportation and translation services when needed, so the prospective parents don't have to worry about such things.

If you have a good agency, your adoption process will be fine. This doesn't mean you won't have interruptions and setbacks, and it doesn't mean you won't sometimes feel as though you're on the precipice of complete disaster. It will just mean that you won't, in all likelihood, *actually* be on the precipice of complete disaster. With an agency, you needn't worry that you're going to shipwreck the whole process by forgetting a key piece of paper or violating some state law unknown to you. Your agency is watching for such things. With this the case, you can simply give yourself over to prayer and to filling out the papers, conducting the interviews, etc. as your agency directs you to do.

Christians thinking about adoption often ask me if it is necessary to use a Christian agency to adopt. There are several reasons why a Christian agency can be helpful. Christian agency personnel will understand, for instance, your convictions on parenting and will be able to provide counsel about how best to help your new children adapt to your home, once the adoption is completed. A Christian agency is often able to provide genuine ministry to birth mothers and orphans waiting to be adopted. In this case, then, you are helping to support a missionary agency that offers more than psychological care for those involved.

Furthermore, a Christian agency will anticipate any possible religious liberty complications to your adoption. They can counsel you, for instance, if a social worker balks at your Christian convictions (as we'll see, though, this is rarely, if ever, the case). In the case of international adoptions, they'll know where there are religious tensions that might be relevant. One of the most tension-filled moments of our adoption came when I gave my occupation information to the judge in Russia. "Baptist minister," I said with a clump of phlegm in my throat. Missionaries in the region had told us that Baptists and Pentecostals were considered by many in the area to be a "cult." Some even believed, we were told, that Baptists practiced ritual child sacrifice, including the devouring of the firstborn. After announcing my occupation as asked, I licked my lips, chapped by nervous anxiety, and then immediately stopped, fearful that I would look to the dour judge as though I were hungrily anticipating the feast of baby flesh awaiting me. As it turns out, the judge didn't care about my Baptist identity. Still, a Christian agency could have prepared me for what to do if she had.

Even so, the most important thing about your agency is not whether or not it is identified as Christian, but whether or not it is competent and experienced. We tried to use a well-respected evangelical Christian adoption agency, but the agency was experiencing some hiccups in its certification in some countries overseas at the time. They recommended the secular agency we used, an agency certified and experienced in overseas adoption. It turned out that this agency sponsored a seminar in a church near us, a church we knew and respected.

This is the best way to find an agency, through simple word of mouth. If you know couples who have adopted, ask them what agency they used and how they liked it. Attend adoption seminars when you see them advertised in churches and community centers around your town. There you can talk face-to-face with agency representatives and, often, families who have adopted. If your church belongs to a denomination or fellowship of churches, call the headquarters of your group and ask if anyone there can recommend a good agency, or contact a church in your tradition with experience in guiding families to a good agency.

Once you've located an agency, you might ask the staff for some families who have used that organization in the past and who wouldn't mind talking to you about their experience with the agency. Get a sense of how the agency personnel deal with questions, especially routine questions from nervous applicants. After all, your agency representatives will be the ones reassuring you through the process when you think (and you *will* think this), "Everything's falling apart." If you're adopting internationally, your agency personnel will be the ones perhaps receiving calls in the middle of the night, though it is the middle of the business day wherever you are in the world. Asking a series of "what would you do if" questions (for example, "What would you do if a birth mother changed her mind about adoption at the last minute?") can reassure you about the problem-solving ability of the agency personnel and of their patience for the kinds of questions you'll have as the process moves forward.

The legal requirements for adoption are going to change from jurisdiction to jurisdiction, but most adoptions are going to require what's called a "home study." This strikes fear in the hearts of many prospective parents. Part of this fear is entirely natural. "The parental screening requirement is a very real deterrent to many who might otherwise consider adoption," writes a Harvard law professor. "People don't like to become helpless supplicants, utterly dependent on the grace of social workers, with respect to something as basic as their desire to become parents."[2] That's true. Being evaluated by a social worker to see if you're "fit" to be parents can be humiliating. This is especially true for Christians who've spent long hours studying the Scriptures and preparing themselves to be parents and now are being questioned by a stranger on these matters. Sometimes adopting parents are resentful when they hear of gum-popping teenagers becoming pregnant in a three-minute act of passion while they, mature believers, have to fill out questionnaires detailing their emotions about their childhood family vacations.

Add to this, though, some particular angst among conservative Christians who are expecting the "culture wars" to come to their house in the form of an adoption home study. The stereotype of a social worker, after all, is that he or she is probably not serving cookies and punch at Vacation Bible School on days off. We may fear that the social worker is there precisely to keep children away from what he or she perceives to be "fundamentalists" like us.

Some adopting couples have probably had ideological skir-

---

[2]Elizabeth Bartholet, *Family Bonds: Adoption, Infertility, and the New World of Child Production* (Boston: Beacon, 1999), 34.

mishes with their social workers, though I've talked with hundreds of adoptive parents and I've yet to see a case of this. It may be that, in the future, evangelical Christians and traditionalist Roman Catholics and Eastern Orthodox parishioners will be ruled ineligible to adopt, but we're far from that time now. Your social worker isn't there to evaluate you theologically or politically. He or she is there to make sure your home isn't a danger to children and that you're not presenting symptoms of mental illness or deranged behavior. The social worker wants to make sure you don't live with shards of glass on the floor of your living room, that you don't have posters of serial killers on the wall, and that you and your spouse aren't on the verge of divorce. The social worker will be looking to see if you have smoke alarms, rails on staircases, fences around swimming pools, and so forth. It is a relatively painless and, in many cases, pleasant experience. In our situation, I left the interviews thankful for the social worker and praying God's blessing on her service in this role.

It is true that your social worker may see things very differently from the way you do, especially on matters of discipline. Your social worker may give you advice about parenting, and some of the advice may sound insane to you. One of the social workers with whom we interviewed recommended that we not use negative words, such as no, with the children. She counseled that we find positive ways to rephrase things so as to avoid "breaking the child's will." I asked her what we should do if the child were doing something we thought could be dangerous, and she replied, "Well, sometimes it's good to find things to distract the child like, say, a big red ball." When she left, I told my wife, "I do not ever want to be caught in a dark alley with that woman's children." Maria quipped, "At least not without a big red ball." The social worker saw the task of parenting differently than we did, but it wasn't a confrontation. She was offering counsel—from her perspective and her experience—not giving dictates from the state.

It's very, very important that you and your spouse agree from the beginning to tell the truth to your social worker and every other legitimate authority involved in the adoption process. If you are asked about how you plan to rear the child religiously, about your behavior expectations, about your disciplinary philosophy, whatever you're asked, give an honest answer. This doesn't mean that you need to say everything you believe to the social worker or other officials. Most faithful Christians believe in some form of restrained, intentional, corporal discipline. Most social workers do not. When asked about discipline, it is acceptable to say, in the words of a friend of mine who has adopted several children, "We believe in firm but loving age-appropriate discipline." If asked directly about spanking, I believe an adopting couple should answer directly.

The same principle is at work if you are interviewing with a birth mother who is evaluating whether or not you should adopt her child. Christians can debate whether or not lying is permissible in certain instances to save a life. I don't think the Hebrew midwives sinned when they saved the babies from Pharaoh by telling him that the Jewish women were too quick in giving birth for their babies to be caught (Ex. 1:17–20). I don't think Rahab sinned when she told the soldiers the Israelite spies weren't there (Josh. 2; Heb. 11:31). I don't think Corrie ten Boom was sinning when she lied to Nazi troops about hidden Jewish refugees. Whatever you think though about whether it's ever acceptable to lie in such desperate life-or-death situations, you won't be in one of those situations in this process. God is not going to bless you for saying things that aren't true. Answer every question honestly and with the grace and tenderness of the Lord Jesus.

The paperwork you'll have to do isn't advanced calculus, but you'll want to use wise discernment in organizing the process. Put the most organized person in the household in charge of making sure all the paperwork is done in a timely fashion. This is typically the one who keeps the checkbook in your household division of labor. Most of the organization required is simply waiting for papers to arrive, showing the other spouse where to sign, and having documents notarized by a notary public at one's local bank.

Keep yourself from being overwhelmed by the sheer volume of all this paperwork by seeing it for what it is, a labor for the children God is calling to be yours. You are kind of like Jacob of old, working years of arduous labor for the permission from her father to marry Rachel (Gen. 29:1–30). For Jacob, the years of work "seemed to him but a few days because of the love he had for her" (v. 20). You won't have to do backbreaking servitude in the Middle Eastern desert sun for your child. It won't last seven years, much less fourteen, as in Jacob's case. But for you too it will be worth it. And like a woman who doesn't remember her labor pains after she sees her child, you'll hardly remember the frustrations of bureaucracy after your child is on your lap at home.

Fill out the paperwork "with a good will as to the Lord and not to man" (Eph. 6:5–7). Yes, some of the paperwork and some of the exercises are overlapping, mindless, and trivial. Imagine, though, that Jesus himself is asking you to fill out this stuff, and do it with joyfulness and gratitude.

FINANCES

Can you put a baby on Visa or MasterCard? How can you afford to adopt when it's so expensive? This is often one of the first questions I'm asked by couples interested in adoption. Can we afford it? Is adoption something only economically affluent people can pull off? Will this process bankrupt us for a generation or more?

First of all, yes, adoption is expensive. Some adoptions can be very expensive. But let's put the cost in perspective. Have you ever been to a parenting seminar where an expert starts talking about money? Have you heard these experts rattle off the figure of what it takes to raise a child from birth to eighteen? It sounds daunting, doesn't it? When you hear a figure like that, you don't think of anything else on which you could ever spend that amount of cash. It sounds like something only a hyper-wealthy entrepreneur could afford. But look around. There are parents everywhere. They're not all Rockefellers or Hiltons. They're not all tycoons or heiresses. Garbage collectors have children, as do discount store shelf-stockers and coffee shop clerks and people in every other occupation you can imagine. Child-rearing itself is expensive, but all kinds of people do it—because it's a priority, and families adjust their internal economies to fit.

The same is true with adoption. When you hear the cost of an adoption—and the costs differ wildly depending on the kind of adoption, where it is, and so forth—you'll be tempted to despair. That money, though, is a final figure, with everything accounted for, in most cases. The money isn't rung up on a cash register at the end as someone scans your baby's leg across an electronic reader. The cost is dribbled out a little bit at a time across the entire process—an attorney's fee here, an agency's fee there, an airline ticket here, a birth mother's hospital bill there, and so forth.

Financial stewardship is important, for Christians more so than for others. Jesus tells us, after all, that anyone building a tower or planning a war first counts the cost to see if he has what it takes to pull it off successfully (Luke 14:25–32).

At the same time, though, Jesus never reduces stewardship to a green eyeshade kind of dollars and cents calculation. Judas Iscariot seemed to be a wise steward of God's resources when he questioned Mary's decision to pour a bottle of expensive perfume onto the feet of Jesus. Wouldn't it make better sense, as Judas pointed out, to sell such a product and use it for ministry to the poor? Jesus, though, affirmed the extravagance—and seeming ridiculousness—of Mary's stewardship over the seemingly more rational stewardship of Judas (John 12:1–8).

Some Christians have firm convictions against any kind of debt. Because the Bible tells us that "the borrower is the slave of the lender" (Prov. 22:7), these Christians believe nothing should be purchased that can't be paid for in cash. In an era when so many people, including Christians, are awash in indebtedness to credit cards and car payments and so on, I respect those Christians who reject debt altogether. If you're of this conviction, then don't violate your conscience. Most Christians, though, don't believe the Bible forbids all debt, just unwise and enslaving forms of it. Most Christians, for instance, will take out a mortgage for a home and don't believe they are unwise stewards for doing so. If you fit in this category, I do not think taking out a loan for the purpose of adoption is wrong—provided, as in all things, you've wisely considered how you're going to pay off the money you've borrowed.

At a more fundamental level, it's important to know that you don't always have to know how God will equip you to adopt before you begin praying and planning toward adoption. I know it's a Christian cliché to shrug and say, "God will provide" in the face of financial uncertainty, but the reason it's a cliché is because God does indeed provide. Now, to be sure, God doesn't promise to bless us with material prosperity, and he doesn't indulge us with money to cover our foolish consumerist binges. But God repeatedly provides the means for willing men and women to become parents, including those he's called to adopt, even though sometimes, at first, it seems economically impossible.

For some of you, adoption means you'll need to get your economic house in order. You may need to pay off your credit cards, maybe work some extra hours at your job, perhaps sell your new car and replace it with a used one, consider canceling your cable television, limit your nights out at restaurants or movies. There are many ways of storing up resources without ruining your life. This kind of discipline for the sake of another is precisely what you'll need to be a parent anyway, and it might as well start with your bank statement. Do not go into debt to finance an adoption if you're already perilously in debt with unwieldy student loans or credit card debt and so forth. Consider your responsibility to get your debts in order as part of the adoption cost itself.

For others of you, adoption means you'll need to learn to have things done for you by others. Adoption, as we'll discuss later in this book, can't be an individual family working alone. Adoption is such a big project that it entails a broader community. In many instances, this affects the economic aspect of the decision as well.

When Maria and I started the adoption process, we had no money. I was a doctoral student, working as a part-time research assistant, and my wife was a very low-paid office secretary. In our living room was a threadbare couch we had bought for about thirty dollars. After we purchased it, we had to spend another fifteen dollars to get the marijuana smoke smell out of it from the previous owners' use. My car was a rusted little Subaru with an overheating radiator that could only get me about a mile and a half down the road without needing a gallon of water poured into it. We lived off our meager salaries and the money I'd earn preaching in little country churches on the weekend. Later in the process, I was appointed to a seminary faculty, but even so, the financial weight of the adoption was overwhelming to think about. I don't like worrying about how I'm going to pay for things, and I can't stand the idea of being indebted to anyone. And yet God was, it seemed, leading us to do something that would cost possibly more than the two of us combined made in a year.

One day I looked up from my office desk to see a young man peering in the window of my door. I recognized him. He was a youth minister from a church in another state. I welcomed him, thinking he wanted counsel about some pastoral situation in his church or some doctrinal point in the Bible he couldn't understand. Instead, after a few minutes of idle conversation, he looked at me and said, "My wife and I were left some money from a relative who passed away. It's about ten thousand dollars, and we were going to use it one day to go toward a down payment on a house." I nodded, trying to anticipate what the ethical dilemma would be for which he was seeking my "wisdom." He said, "My wife and I have been blessed with children, and I know you are trying to adopt. We want you to have this money and use it toward the adoption of your children."

I wasn't expecting that, and I quickly dismissed it. "Oh no,"

I said. "I appreciate that greatly, but I want you and your wife to use that money for your house or for your kids' college education." I assured him of my appreciation and politely changed the subject to something else, trying to avoid the awkwardness of the moment.

"Are you telling me you already have all the money on hand that you need for the adoption?" he asked. "It's already paid for?" I said, "Well, no, but . . ." This young minister interrupted me. "Well, then, I'm sorry to be disrespectful, but this isn't really about you," he said. "I mean, we aren't in a place where we can adopt right now, but we want to be a part of adoption. We think God is calling us to this. And it seems to me as though maybe you're too, I don't know, prideful or something to receive this." I blinked. He looked me in the eye and said, "Maybe you just need to repent of your pride and self-confidence and just let somebody bless you."

He was, at that moment, the prophet pointing his finger—"Thou art the man"—exposing the slimy recesses of my heart, right there under the fluorescent ceiling lamps of my office. I had nothing to say. It was true that I was embarrassed at the thought of taking money from someone else. I wasn't anybody's welfare recipient. I'd paid for every car I'd ever owned with cash. I'd worked my own way through all my schooling. I paid off every credit card bill I'd ever had in full the month it was due. I didn't like the idea of this young man's family knowing he was giving the money—money they'd like him to have for his family—to me. I didn't like having the roles reversed on me suddenly, sitting there as a supplicant to be helped rather than a sage to be consulted. It was humiliating.

This young man looked at my tear-streamed face and said, "Well, I'll mail the check tomorrow." He continued, "I just want two conditions met. We'd like a picture of the boys every once in a while as they're growing up. I also want to make sure no one ever knows who I am. You can tell people that someone helped you, if you think it'll help people do the same. But I don't want anyone ever to know it was I who did it. I want God to get all the glory here. I don't want any."

His gift was a huge portion of the cost of the adoption. Soon after that, our friends took up a special offering among them for another large chunk of the cost. My grandmother loaned us some money, interest-free, to cover some more. I couldn't—and wouldn't—have planned any of that. God was providing for us financially, and he was humbling some of what was exalted in my life in the process.

Years later, I told this story to a pastor friend. He pointed out a line in a song by my favorite songwriter, Michael Card. Singing about Jesus washing his disciples' feet, a living parable of Christian community, Card says, "One will kneel. And one will yield."[3] My friend said, "Isn't that the way it is? Jesus humbled himself to kneel and wash feet. But the problem was that Peter was too prideful to receive it. You were too. Sometimes it takes more holiness to receive than to give."

Think of how humiliating it must have been for the Jerusalem church to receive an offering collected from congregations in Galatia and Corinth (1 Cor. 16:1–4). After all, Jerusalem was the mother church, in the City of the Great King. This church was rescued, kept in survival, by uncircumcised Gentiles. What kind of great God is this, who delights in such paradoxes, in pulling down the mighty and lifting up the humble? Maybe through the adoption process, God seeks to do the same for you. Maybe he's drawing you to give money, freely and anonymously. Maybe he's drawing you to receive it. Maybe he's seeking to sanctify you in the process.

Whatever the case is for you, pray for God's provision. Enlist others in your congregation to pray with you for financial empowerment. God is a Father, not a landlord. If God means for you to adopt, he'll give you what you need to do so.

WAITING FOR THE CALL

For me, the hardest part of the adoption process was the decision to do it in the first place. For my wife, the most difficult aspect was

[3]Michael Card, "The Basin and the Towel," *Poiema*, Sparrow Records, 1994.

the wait. If God is calling you to adopt, you may well have a time of waiting. Sometimes the wait can be quite short—weeks or months. In some cases, it can be a year or more, if a birth mother is difficult to locate or if the country from which you're adopting experiences political trouble. In almost any case, it will seem to be a long time as you wait for the call telling you that your child or children are ready for you.

This waiting can wear on a family, especially on a couple who've come to adoption after tragedies such as infertility or miscarriages. Sometimes adopting parents can even exhibit physical symptoms from anxiety. I've known people with chronic headaches, stomach problems, heart palpitations—even someone who wound up in a hospital emergency room thinking he was having a heart attack—while waiting for adoptions to go through. In all these instances, it was simply their bodies reacting to the stress. In all these cases there was nothing wrong. It was just the uncertainty of it.

You may feel—especially if you're a man—as though you ought to be fighting someone for your children's lives. But there's no one to fight. You may feel as though you should be doing something to hurry along the process, even after all your paperwork is done. But there's nothing more to do.

This sensation isn't unique to adoption. God has designed the universe around us so that anticipation is built into the order of things. Even in the most typical situations, after all, God doesn't create babies out of nothing. A woman may cry out from the bathroom, "Guess what, honey? The test says I'm pregnant!" but only rarely does a woman cry out from the bathroom, "Guess what, honey? I just gave birth!" God slowly knits together a child in the womb as his parents wait for his arrival.

God does this in almost every aspect of life. He didn't blink the universe together in an instant but instead called it together, piece by piece, over the space of six days. Even when God created humanity as the crown of his universe, he made Adam wait for his queen, creating anticipation for her by showing him in the world around him that "there was not found a helper fit for him" (Gen. 2:20). At the ascension of Jesus, his disciples wondered if it was "at this time" that he would "restore the kingdom to Israel" (Acts 1:6). Instead, for thousands of years, so far, the gospel has gone forth through the invisible dynamism of the Spirit, while we wait still for Jesus to appear in the eastern skies.

There's something about patience that God deems necessary for our life in the age to come. And so, whether through agriculture or discipleship or bodily development or eschatology or procreation, God makes us wait. And he makes us into the kind of people who can wait. We rejoice in such things, Paul tells us, because we know that "suffering produces endurance, and endurance produces character, and character produces hope" (Rom. 5:3–4). Our adoption in Christ involves patient waiting, hopeful anticipation (Rom. 8:24–25). In the earthly scenario of adoption, as in the heavenly experience of our own adoption, we "hope for what we do not see" because we "wait for it with patience" (Rom. 8:25).

While you're waiting, spend time cultivating the spiritual disciplines you'll need as parents. After all, you'll be waiting again someday. It might be on a Friday night when you don't know where your rebel child is at 3 in the morning. It might be in a hospital waiting room as you flip through magazines waiting to hear from the doctors if the transplant was successful. It might be as you sit by the phone, hoping to hear from the battlefield where your baby is serving as a soldier. Learn now to pray with dependence. Pray together as you wait for the protection of your child. Pray for his future salvation. Pray for your own wisdom to lead your child toward godliness.

Spend this time preparing your family and friends for the new arrival. Adopting couples are sometimes surprised by how the people in their lives react to adoption, both positively and negatively. Some family members I expected to be completely apathetic to the adoption were tracking the days with us, almost as excited as we were. Another family member was cold to the whole idea, changing the subject whenever Maria brought it up with her on the phone. She eventually, and inexplicably, warmed up to the idea—and to the boys—as soon as we received the call to get them. I suppose she was "protecting" herself from getting too excited, in case it all fell through. You may find similar situations among your family and friends. Bear patiently with them. If they love you, they'll come around.

Sometimes social workers or adoption agencies will tell adopting parents to keep grandparents and other extended family members away for the first three to six weeks (or even longer) after a child has been adopted. This is to give parents time to bond with the child. In some of the more dire circumstances—a child who has been through major trauma such as abuse, etc. in recent days—this may be appropriate. In the vast majority of situations, though, such advice is misguided. We don't bond in isolation from others; we bond together in community. You don't want to overwhelm your child with new faces, but you want him or her to know that he or she is part of a larger family now of people who love him or her. You also don't want to rob grandparents and aunts and uncles of the opportunity to be a part of your child's life from the beginning. An arrival home from adoption is very much like a birth. There's no shame to this. Don't treat it clinically. Allow your loved ones to celebrate with you.

Often friends will want to have a baby shower for the adopting mother. This is, of course, appropriate, just as it would be for a pregnant mother. It can be complicated, though, not only by the unpredictability of the adoption process. Sometimes a family not only doesn't know whether they're "having a boy or a girl" but also whether they're having an infant or a toddler. Sometimes, too, a baby shower can add anxiety to an already worried mother, if it happens too soon for her. She may wonder, "What will I do with all these gifts if the adoption falls through?" In these cases, a husband ought to discern his wife's best interest and help their friends decide whether to go ahead or wait on the shower.

Even when there's some uncertainty, though, a baby shower can be helpful in the waiting process. After all, the fears of (especially first-time) adopting families are, in the vast majority of cases, unfounded. The baby shower can be a time for family and friends to pray for the family and for the quick resolution of the adoption process. The shower, or a dinner in honor of the new family, can also be an excellent way for family and friends to be reminded of the gospel archetype of adoption. Such things can spur on others who can adopt to start praying about whether God wants the next baby shower to be theirs.

CONCLUSION

One's life story is typically made up of little decisions. Think about how different your life would be now if you hadn't made a decision, maybe one you came to in a matter of seconds. Think about all the decisions made for you—decisions that you probably never noticed or thought about—decisions that have formed who you are and what you're doing. If your grandfather hadn't noticed that girl at the picnic or if he'd been too shy to say anything to her, you wouldn't exist. All of human history is like that. Providence moves forward mysteriously as God works through billions of seemingly inconsequential decisions. "If one Egyptian tailor hadn't cheated on the threads of Joseph's mantle, Potiphar's wife would never had been able to tear it, present it as evidence to Potiphar that Joseph attacked her, gotten him thrown in prison, and let him be in a position to interpret Pharaoh's dream, win his confidence, advise him to store seven years of grain, and save his family, the seventy original Jews from whom Jesus came," apologist Peter Kreeft writes. "We owe our salvation to a cheap Egyptian tailor."[4]

If God is moving you toward adoption, you'll need to make some decisions at the outset. The hardest decision, if you've decided to adopt, has already been made. The most important thing for you to know about these decisions is that whatever you decide, you're not going to wreck God's plan for your life. Whatever your views

---

[4]Peter Kreeft, C. S. Lewis for the Third Millennium: Six Essays on The Abolition of Man (San Francisco: Ignatius, 1994), 61.

about how God's kingship fits with human freedom, you know as a Christian that God is at work in bringing about his good purposes for you. Your decisions fit, mysteriously, into that overall plan. Don't worry. As you move forward, remember that your God is king; so "do not be anxious" (Matt. 6:25–34). Just as our Father provides food for the birds of the air, he also provides them with nests and hatching eggs.

6

Jim Crow in the Church Nursery

How to Think about Racial Identity, Health Concerns, and Other Uncomfortable Adoption Questions

SHE ACTUALLY HAD a measuring tape, for a baby's head. I didn't know who this woman was, but I was disgusted. When we began the adoption process, we knew only a handful of people who had adopted, and we knew no one who had adopted from overseas. It was jarring then, after landing in Russia, to talk to other Americans who had come to Russia to adopt. The woman with the measuring tape said she wanted to measure the craniums of their potential children "to make sure there is nothing wrong with them." Another told us that this was her third—and final—trip. The first two adoption referrals she had received had severe and obvious "attachment issues," and she had turned down the children. It seemed to me that she was sizing up these children as though she was sorting through a litter of puppies or browsing through a line of secondhand refrigerators.

She spoke with hushed tones as she spoke of how horrible her last visit to the orphanage had been. The child she rejected had "something wrong with her," this lady just knew, because the girl had a "blank stare" in her eyes. "You know?" the woman prodded. "Like, you know, the lights are on, but maybe nobody's home?" I ventured that maybe the little girl had a "blank stare" because she'd been staring at a blank wall for twelve hours a day, but the lady assured me I just didn't understand how bad it could be.

If the Lord calls you to adopt, you'll probably be asked about the kind of child you want to adopt. Your agency or facilitator will probably ask your preferences about the age and sex of the child you'd like to adopt. They'll ask whether you're applying to adopt one child or if you're open to a sibling group. And then they may ask you some questions that are really uncomfortable—such as the race of a child you'd like to adopt and whether you want a "healthy" or "special-needs" child.

Some of these decisions, again, will be made for you, in the way providence works together for your good. Some of these decisions, though, you'll have to make, and they can raise some of the rawest questions of your Christian witness in general and your calling as an adopting parent in particular. Some of these decisions are also fraught with ethical complexities. Am I a horrible person if I adopt a child of another race? What will my extended family think if I spend all this money to adopt a special-needs baby who might not live to see next Christmas? Such things bring opportunities to see the glory of our Lord Jesus.

A BOY OR A GIRL?

Whenever a woman announces she's pregnant, one of the first questions asked is, "Are you hoping for a boy or a girl?" Thankfully, parents don't yet—at least not on a widespread scale—have the ability to make this godlike decision for their children. Many who thought they'd die without a little girl can't imagine their lives now without their son, and vice versa. Sometimes adopting parents, too, are asked by agencies or other adoption facilitators to specify whether they'd like to adopt a girl or a boy.

For some of you this decision will be made for you. We told our agency we'd be happy with either boys or girls or one of each. Our agency representative told us we'd just made a decision to adopt boys, since the vast majority of other applicants to adopt from this part of the world wanted girls. When we asked why, we were told people tend to think girls are easier to rear. I can certainly see why someone would think this, when I compare my rambunctious, testosterone-surging, wrestling, running-through-the-house (with scissors if they could reach them) males to the gentle, demurely smiling, patiently sitting young females in other households. My friends with both sons and daughters laugh at the notion that girls are easier to raise. As one put it, "Sure, girls are easier . . . for the first ten years. Then the difficulty level reverses. Parenting is hard, and the sex of your child isn't going to make that any less true."

Those adopting from cultures in which women are traditionally devalued will find their situation the exact reverse of ours. A decision to leave the sex of the child open to God's providence will usually in that case mean a daughter. In either case, Christians have an opportunity to care for those unwanted either because of their allegedly "incorrigible" maleness or their allegedly "inferior" femaleness. In all of this, Christians must remember that in our adoption as sons, "there is no male and female" (Gal. 3:28). God is imaged in both little girls and little boys. Both are equally precious in his sight. They should be in ours as well.

A NEWBORN OR AN OLDER CHILD?

Adopting parents are also sometimes asked to choose the age of the child they seek to adopt. Again, sometimes this decision is made by divine providence—if you're waiting for a birth mother to give birth, for instance, or if you're the foster parent of a twelve-year-old child God's calling you to adopt. In other instances, though, the decision is up to you. A Christian worldview comes into this decision, whichever way you decide.

As we'll discuss a bit later, a Christian understanding of the world sees a child's character not as genetically determined but as shaped to a significant degree by parental discipleship and discipline. The younger the child is, the more opportunity you will have to bring up that child in Christian nurture and instruction, to form the character and eternal destiny of this son or daughter. An adopting Christian couple may decide they want to adopt an infant or young toddler so as to exercise a maximal amount of stewardship in that child's life. That's a legitimate decision.

On the other hand, Christians also must acknowledge that the older a child is, the less "adoptable" he is. It is always easier for orphanages or agencies to find willing adopting parents for cute newborns than for older children. Think about how awkward you were at certain ages of your preadolescent and adolescent life. I shudder to see videotaped images of myself as a twelve- to fourteen-year-old, sitting sullenly and awkwardly in my chair, glaring at my father as he tried out his new camera . . . again. No one would have wanted to adopt this kid. By the time a child has pimples, he's less "sellable" to families who swoon over adorability. By the time a child has erections or menstrual cycles, he or she becomes "scary" to families, families that now see him or her as another unpredictable adult rather than as a son or daughter.

Some Christian families are called to adopt older children, especially families with some age and experience. This doesn't mean it will be easy—far from it. Older children in an orphanage or foster care system have sometimes been deeply wounded, even traumatized. Such trauma is not easily undone, even by parental love. The gospel, though, is more powerful than childhood trauma. After all, we know, "while we were still weak, at the right time Christ died for the ungodly" (Rom. 5:6). We know that "while we were enemies we were reconciled to God by the death of his Son" (Rom. 5:10). Some Christian families, perhaps even some reading this book, are called to show that kind of sacrificial courage in the life of an older child, maybe even a pot-smoking, profanity-spewing prodigal. By no means are all, or even most, older adopted children described in this way, but this caricature represents a worst-case scenario, a scenario some of you may be called to transform with the presence of Christ.

ONE CHILD OR SIBLINGS?

Maria and I went from the parents of no children to the parents of two children overnight, and it was all an accident, at least humanly speaking. A line on our agency questionnaire recommended that we be certified through our home study for two children, should there be a sibling pairing. We did so, though expecting only to adopt one child. One day though, while working in my office, I suddenly had an unexplained urge to pray for a sibling group. I called Maria and said, "I'm praying for two babies. What do you think?" She said, "Well, you know that's up to us. We can adopt two babies if we want." I blurted out, "Let's do it!" She was excited but reticent. "You know that will cost more money." I didn't care. It just seemed right.

Sometimes agencies or adoption facilitators will ask whether you're interested in adopting one or multiple children—perhaps even a sibling group—at the same time. This decision has everything to do with how you're equipped emotionally and financially. It also has to do with your housing arrangements and things as mundane as whether there's room in your home for more than one crib or bed.

Adoption can be expensive, and adopting more than one child usually raises the cost dramatically. Still, families who plan to adopt more than one child in the future sometimes find it's better stewardship (especially if it's an international adoption, which includes expenses like plane tickets and overseas housing arrangements) to adopt more than one child at the same time. It is often a good idea, if you are at all able to handle it, to go through the process to be able to adopt more than one child, should something happen at the last minute (maybe you discover there's a brother or sister you didn't know about) in your adoption that throws your plans askew.

Our "accidental" decision to adopt two children was precisely the right decision for us. It wouldn't be right for everyone. We'd never had children before; so raising two didn't seem like any additional work to us. It just seemed normal. It wasn't until we had our third son, Samuel, who went through his two- and three-year-old phases alone, that we realized how much easier it could be. Having two also kept us from "spoiling" either one of them with hovering attention. We were just too busy keeping fingers out of wall sockets and jelly from flying against the wall to be smothering parents.

More importantly, the two of them were obviously meant to be brothers. They were in the same orphanage room together, probably from near birth, and they have been inseparable friends ever since. When I ask whether they'd like ice cream, Timothy looks to Benjamin to see what kind he should order. At night, it's hard to keep them in their own beds; they always seem to wind up in the same one, curled up together. And if one is in trouble—like last night while I was typing this chapter and one sneaked out of his bed to creep around the house—the other one is right behind him. Two (or more!) children at once might not be the right decision for you, should the Lord lead you to adopt, but it's something to pray through beforehand.

DOES RACE MATTER?

I can't tell if you're white, black, Latino, or whatever as you read this page. It doesn't matter. Up to this point, the gospel is the gospel and adoption is adoption. But what if, as you proceed toward adoption, someone were to ask you your racial preference for your child? Should you have such a preference? Suppose you're an African-American couple—should you specify a black child? If you're Caucasian, should you make sure you don't adopt a child who is a person of color?

Some people would tell you that transracial adoption is wrong. I'm not just talking about bigoted white people either. Every few years a group of social workers or adoption experts will issue a warning about adopting children of a different ethnicity or cultural background than the adopting parents. While no studies have proven any kind of psychological or social harm in children so adopted, some reports have noted, "these children often face major challenges as the only person of color in an all-white environment, trying to cope with being different."[1] I suppose the same would be the case for a white child in an African-American or Latino family, though to a much lesser degree since, at least in North America, their ethnicity

---

[1] Ron Nixon, "De-Emphasis on Race in Adoption Is Criticized," *New York Times*, May 27, 2008, A-15.

would be the majority culture and they wouldn't face a centuries-long backlog of racial discrimination.

Most opponents of transracial adoption don't argue for an outright legal ban on the practice. Some organizations of social workers have argued, for instance, that race should be one factor among many when determining where to place children. That seems reasonable. If a Latino family is available to adopt a Latino child, that should be part of the decision-making process. If we lived in a world in which there were an abundance of prospective parents for every child, that might be reasonable. Instead, though, we live in an era in which yet another layer of bureaucracy is yet another barrier to many children's finding homes at all. "Parents' attitudes toward transracial adoption have become much more liberal since the 1970s, but the racial attitudes of social workers, those sometimes pitiless gatekeepers on the adoption pilgrimage, have hardened," writes Kevin Williamson. He concludes that "the matchmakers at the heart of the adoption system are part of the problem."[2]

Others, though, believe transracial adoption in almost any case is dangerous and wrong and seek to stop it either through legal means or through social disapproval. Some persons who were adopted across racial and ethnic lines have raised concerns. Some of them have gone so far as to assert that they were not adopted but "abducted" by those who sought to steal their cultural heritage from them. Some particularly opinionated opponents of transracial adoption have gone so far as to label it an act of cultural genocide.

On the one hand, there seems to be some validity to this concern. After all, there's no such thing as a "citizen of the world." We all come from somewhere, and the kind of rootlessness that contemporary hyper-capitalist globalization has brought to our culture atrophies the human spirit. Too many of us have, in the words of singer Don Williams, "learned to talk like the man on the six o'clock news."[3] There's a sameness about us, with regional accents, ethnic

---

[2]Kevin D. Williamson, "Lost Generation," *National Review*, August 4, 2008, 37.
[3]Don Williams, "Good Ole Boys Like Me," MCA Nashville, 1987.

dialects, and cultural traditions all swept aside for a world made safe for McDonald's and mass-produced pop music. It's probably impossible to quantify just how damaging this current age of hypermobility and commercialized sameness is to our happiness.

It's also hard to overestimate the legacy of racial hatred and bigotry. It's easy for the white American majority to speak of a "colorblind" nation, but we're not more than a generation removed from color-segregated water fountains in the town where I sit typing this right now.

Moreover, some of our attitudes toward transracial adoption have, in fact, been shaped by a paternalistic view of the whole thing. Popular culture in the 1970s and 1980s sent downstream a view of transracial adoption that was trivializing at best, condescending at worst. Movie audiences roared with laughter when comedian Steve Martin narrated the opening scene of the movie *The Jerk*: "I was born a poor black child." The idea of a white man being raised by black parents seemed patently ridiculous to moviegoers, not like the cute black kids they saw on their weekly television situation comedies. That made sense since those kids were "lucky" to come into such white privilege. As the theme song to one seventies TV program put it, "A man is born, he's a man of means. Then along come two, and they've got nothing but their jeans." Or was it "their genes"? I couldn't tell, and it didn't really matter. They had "different strokes," and that was what moved the world.

It's true also that non-minority parents sometimes don't know all the subtle ways their minority children will face discrimination. Scholar Sandra Patton writes about an African-American woman named Kristin who was adopted by white parents. Kristin says her mother would read to her *Little Black Sambo*, a children's book mired in the racist view of black people of the last century's minstrel shows. It's shocking, first of all, that any parent would read this book to a child, but it's even more shocking that Kristin reports that she likes the book. "I don't see what other people see," she says.

Patton concludes, "Her parents did not teach her to recognize racist stereotypes."[4]

Even so, the discouraging of transracial adoption is counterproductive. Yes, we live, even still, in what one transracial adoptee calls "a very race conscious society."[5] But is the solution to discriminate on the basis of race in the adoption process? Is the answer to centuries of racial hostility to keep homes formed, separately but equally, on the basis of the color of skin?

Old George Wallace is an iconic figure in twentieth-century political and social history, memorialized every time the song "Sweet Home Alabama" is played to this day. Wallace was governor of Alabama, a four-time presidential candidate, and a racial demagogue. He promised the people of his state, and around the country, that he'd maintain "segregation now, segregation tomorrow, segregation forever." And when the courts mandated the integration of public colleges and universities in his state, he vowed to "stand in the schoolhouse door," which he did, at least to pose for the cameras.

Wallace and his segregationist cohorts didn't usually argue their case on the basis of raw racial hatred, at least not openly. Instead they argued that separation was best for both black people and white people. After all, it's human nature to want to be with "one's own kind," to honor one's own traditions, one's own culture.

Wallace's progressive heirs are now using a very similar apologetic for preventing transracial adoption. They're not nearly as crude as the old governor. But they're vowing segregation forever, just like he did. They're standing in the orphanage door. And they too are pretending that they're just being "realistic" about the possibility of racial reconciliation.

Right now there are untold numbers of children—many, many of them from racial minorities—tied up in the foster care system in the United States. Can any of us honestly believe it would be better for an African-American child to remain in this bureaucratic limbo

---

[4]Sandra Patton, *BirthMarks: Transracial Adoption in Contemporary America* (New York: New York University Press, 2000), 72–73.
[5]Nixon, "De-Emphasis on Race in Adoption Is Criticized."

than to be a child to parents whose skin is paler than his? Who could really suggest it would be better for a white Russian child to live in an orphanage until she is dismissed at eighteen to a life of suicide or homelessness or prostitution than for her to grow up with loving African-American parents?

This approach loves the abstract notion of "humanity" more than it loves real, live human beings. It neatly categorizes persons according to their racial lineages rather than according to their need for love, for acceptance, for families. As Christians, we can't see things that way. Our love for neighbor means we must prioritize the need for families for the fatherless, regardless of how their skin colors or languages line up with one another.

Furthermore, for us, there's the issue of the gospel of Jesus Christ. I'm not surprised to see secular social workers or sociologists suggesting that racial identity could be more important than familial love. As we've discussed earlier, in this fallen age it is "natural" to see things according to "the flesh" in that way. The gospel, though, drives us away from that kind of identity in the flesh and toward a new identity, a new family, defined by the Spirit. This new family solidarity is much less visibly obvious. It doesn't make as much sense to the natural man. It's not based on marks in the flesh or melanin levels in the skin or carefully kept genealogies. It's based instead on a Spirit who blows invisibly where he wills, showing up in less visible characteristics such as peace, joy, love, righteousness, gentleness, kindness, self-control.

That's why hesitancy about transracial adoption is so sad. It's not just because some white kids could miss out on some godly black parents or vice versa. It's because it's one more reminder of how we are "conformed to this world" (Rom. 12:2), with all its pitiful divisions.

Yes, parents will have to raise children to contend with whatever challenges may await them. White parents will have to know that in this evil age their beloved African-American son may be called "nigger." Black parents will know that their Asian daughter's classmates may mock her with fake Chinese accents. But is that an obstacle to love, for people who believe the gospel?

This is especially relevant since everyone reading this book, if in Christ, has been transracially adopted. Was it traumatic? Sure. You should see how long it took me to learn Hebrew back in seminary. As I studied those flash cards, on lots of days I wondered if I was cut out to make sense of this strange set of scratchings on the page. But I was learning the language of my forefathers, the children of Abraham, even though I probably don't have an Israelite gene in my bloodstream. But I'm in Christ, and he's Jewish, and, therefore, so am I.

If you're being led toward adoption, it may be that God will send to you a child of a similar ethnicity or skin color. It may be, though, that he will providentially direct you toward a child who looks quite different from you. If you're not sure you can love a child with a different skin color than yours, the first step for you has nothing to do with the adoption process. Repent, and open your heart to love.

For most Christians, though, the issue of racial identity isn't an obstacle. For many of you, instead, the concern is about family members and how they'll react to a child of a different race. I've seen young couples convulsing in tears on the couch in my office, asking how they can love their new child and honor their father and mother at the same time. I've seen family members of every race and every region of the country turn up their noses at the idea of a niece, nephew, or grandchild of another ethnicity, usually with some highly spiritual rhetoric about honoring father and mother or about "the best interest of the child" or a thousand other reasons.

What I'm surprised by is how many of these extended family members are deacons or women's ministry directors or ushers or Sunday school teachers in their churches. They're blissfully unaware, it seems, that what's resting on them is the spirit of antichrist. They seem not to comprehend that their own devotion to their flesh would disqualify non-Semitic folks like them from the promises of God. If Jesus agreed with them on adoption and race, they'd be in hell.

One of the most chilling comments I've ever heard is from an adopting white family told by a relative that he wouldn't have a black child in his family tree. When the young couple gently told the relative he was in sin and that, should he go to heaven, he'll be around a lot of persons of color, the man replied, "Well, then I'll have a long time to learn how to love them." Well, no, sir, you won't have that long. The Bible says you have a very short time—short as a vapor—to learn how to love your brothers and sisters. The Bible tells us, "We know that we have passed out of death into life, because we love the brothers. Whoever does not love abides in death" (1 John 3:14). Moreover, despite what contemporary Christian artwork pictures, Jesus is a Middle Eastern, Galilean Jew. The One you call Lord is a person of color, and his axe is already laid to the root of all our family trees (Matt. 3:10).

The Spirit does indeed command us to honor father and mother (Ex. 20:12). He also tells us, though, that we're to leave father and mother in order to cleave to our spouse, to bring about a new family (Gen. 2:24). Moreover, Jesus tells us that the gospel brings division, sometimes with "father against son and son against father, mother against daughter and daughter against mother, mother-in-law against her daughter-in-law and daughter-in-law against mother-in-law" (Luke 12:53).

Of course, as Paul commands, "so far as it depends on you, live peaceably with all" (Rom. 12:18). But if your parent or grandparent or some other family member rejects your child on the basis of his or her race, then your first responsibility is to your child. What if you gave birth to a baby with a cleft palate or Down's syndrome and your parents were angry about that? The baby, they tell you, wasn't what they were expecting. Would you reject your baby? No; you'd tell your relative, "I'm really sorry you feel this way. But if you can't love my child, you can't love me. We stand or fall together." The same is true here. If your relatives love their bigotry more than your child, speak to them lovingly but directly, just as you would if they were caught in any other sin. But don't give anyone's bigotry veto power over your family.

In many instances where parents or grandparents are overly involved negatively in the adoption process, on the racial question or any other matter, it's because the couple involved has allowed, for years, this kind of benign dictatorship over their lives. It's often comforting to remain somewhat childlike in allowing one's parents or in-laws to retain that kind of paternal power. In some instances, the couple is financially dependent on one set of parents or the other. In this case, the "leave and cleave" mandate needs to be set right before the other issues are addressed.

I hope, if you're reading this book several years after it has been published, that this part doesn't make sense. I hope it seems hopelessly anachronistic to even talk about something like this because such racial hostilities and divisions are so far in the past. I hope that's true. In the meantime, don't fear transracial adoption, whatever the racist relatives or "progressive" experts say. There'll always be secularists—and, sadly, some church people too—who will try to divide us up into neat categories of race and class. Jesus does the opposite, though. He sits us right down at the same table and feeds us bread and wine—together.

HEALTHY OR "SPECIAL-NEEDS"?

It's remarkably easy for those of us without children with disabilities to be judgmental of the people Maria and I encountered in Russia, to shake our heads in disgust at their specifications about their potential child's health and "fitness." But how many people, upon learning they're expecting a baby, pray and ask God for a child with a disability? True, there's a difference here—namely, there are children who already have these disabilities, and they need parents. But nonetheless, it's true that most people would rather have children who are well.

When potential parents begin the adoption process, they're often asked if they'd like to adopt a "healthy" child or a "special-needs" child. Special-needs children could include children with disabilities such as blindness, deafness, cerebral palsy, Down's syndrome, and so forth. A special-needs child might also be a child whose birth mother abused alcohol or drugs during her pregnancy. In some cases, a special-needs adoption might include a child with a life-threatening disease such as AIDS or cancer.

For Christians, the question of children with disabilities is an especially pertinent one. It's not that all Christians called to adopt should adopt children with "something wrong." That's no more the case than the suggestion that all Christians should teach children with disabilities in their local church's Bible study classes. It is true, though, that the followers of Jesus should fill in the gap left by a contemporary Western consumer culture that extends even to the conception and adoption of children. Who better than those who know Christ to welcome the all-too-often unwanted and discarded among the world's orphans? After all, our God himself gathers together "the lame" and "those who have been driven away" and makes "a strong nation" of those who were "cast off" (Mic. 4:6–7). Jesus' gospel is good news for the sick and the disabled. In fact, they are the very ones who make up the marriage feast of our Christ: "the poor and crippled and blind and lame" (Luke 14:21). When we care for the sick and the disabled, Jesus tells us, "you will be blessed, because they cannot repay you. You will be repaid at the resurrection of the just" (Luke 14:14).

Just as you ask God to reveal to you whether he wants you to adopt, pray also that he'll show you whether you should adopt a child with special needs. Often God will place a particular burden in your affections—perhaps for blind children or those with Down's syndrome or fetal alcohol syndrome or AIDS orphans. If you find yourself drawn in your affections and imagination to a particular need, God may be drawing you toward offering yourself as parents to a child in that situation.

There will be times when God will bring you face-to-face with the visage of Jesus in a so-called "special-needs" child. Not long ago

I received a note from a pastor in another state who wrote about an unexpected call he received from an agency through which he and his wife had previously adopted a child. The agency told this pastor about a newborn baby; we'll call him Joey. Everything was set between the birth mother and an adopting couple for Joey to be adopted right after his birth. He was born, though, with a birthmark covering over half of his face. After the couple scheduled to adopt Joey heard about this, they never showed up at the hospital. This pastor and his wife saw the moving of the Holy Spirit in this call, gladly became parents to Joey, and tell me he is a joyful blessing to their home.

The most important factor to keep in mind, though, about the question of special needs is that there is no such thing as a guaranteed healthy child—and it's a good thing too, this side of Zion. God doesn't guarantee healthy children. Any other power attempting such a guarantee would demand a devilish price, to be sure.

It is not necessary that you sign up particularly for a special-needs child if God is calling you to adopt. But if you are not prepared to love and care for a child who is wounded or disabled, should the Lord lead you to such a situation, do not seek marriage (if you're not married yet) or parenthood. I know that statement sounds harsh and perhaps even unkind. But being a father or a mother means caring for a child, whatever his needs and burdens. Your perfectly healthy child could be diagnosed tomorrow with leukemia. Your bicycling little toddler could crumple beneath the weight of a drunk driver's automobile next week. You might not see how you could cope with caring for a sick or wounded child right now, though you know the Lord gives strength when it is needed. If you are unwilling, though, to prepare for such an eventuality, if it comes, then you're not yet prepared to parent, through adoption or the more typical means.

It's also important to note that there's "something wrong" with many children who are adopted, at least at first. If you're adopting internationally, there are regions of the world in which fetal alcohol syndrome is nearly universal because of the way alcohol is used to anesthetize despair in those cultures. Children who have been in orphanages often tend to lag behind "normal kids" simply because they've often not had the kind of nutrition and attention that babies are designed to get. Some countries likewise, by law, can only allow the adoption of "disabled" children, and so these countries will sometimes diagnose their orphans with long lists of ailments, including (in the case of one of our boys) a scary pathological-sounding disorder that turns out to be the medical designation for having endured the "trauma" of passing through a birth canal.

If you'd seen our children the day we arrived home from overseas, they would have looked to you like the sickly babies you sometimes see in documentaries about malnourished Eastern European orphans. By the time their first professional photographs were taken though, almost exactly one month later, they were fat, hardy kids, indistinguishable from the others in the strollers around them in the photographer's line at the department store.

It's true, of course, that children adopted from countries from which Westerners frequently adopt have often lived through some horrible things. It might be expected, then, that these children would be more likely to demonstrate mental health "issues" for the rest of their lives. In fact, it's not. In fact, one report indicates, "children adopted from other countries were *less* likely than domestic adoptees to experience behavioral problems or be referred for mental-health treatment." The researchers postulate this is so because parents willing to adopt from another country may be more "highly motivated to raise children" than others.[6] I can't prove it, but I suspect future studies may show that the same principle is at work in parents adopting from domestic situations, relative to parents in generic samples.

It's true that adopting a child brings with it a certain amount of risk. I know about my biological family's genetic predispositions to heart disease and stroke. I know that I can't think of anyone in my biological family who's ever had breast cancer or muscular dystro-

---

[6]Femmie Juffer and Marinus H. Van Ijzendoorn, *Journal of the American Medical Association*, 293.20 (2005): 2501–2515, cited in "Adoption Options," *Atlantic Monthly*, September 2005, 54.

phy. With my oldest boys, though, I just don't know. You may have numerous charts about family and personal medical history, or you may have nothing at all; but if you adopt a child, there will be a measure of risk. You're just not exactly sure what you're going to get. But isn't that true of every child, uniquely struggling through life with his or her own individual gifts and burdens?

As Amy Laura Hall points out, don't Christians have a Christological grid through which to frame this whole discussion? Isn't it true, as she puts it, that Christians "can be certain that by adopting a human child they will be adopting a creature bearing the *imago Dei*" (the image of God)? Isn't it true also, as she continues, that to fret about our not knowing how a child will "turn out" is in fact "a wrong reading of history, if God is the author of history"?[7]

When I encountered the kind of prospective parents I mentioned earlier, the ones most clamorous for a "healthy child," I was repulsed. I rolled my eyes at the very thought of a measuring tape for a child's skull. But I wasn't one whit holier. I was just as self-protective as they. I just had a more carefully crafted spin. I wouldn't have spoken so crassly about rejecting children, because I had a theology to uphold and a peer group who would've held me accountable if I'd started talking about a child as if I were buying a condominium. But I dreaded as much as any pagan in that airport the thought of struggling for years with a child with a debilitating disease.

On our first trip to Russia, though, after we'd spent several days getting to know these young boys in the orphanage, we received some stomach-twisting news. Our translator told us that it had been previously overlooked that the older boy, Maxim, evidenced in his blood work, at birth, a severe strand of hepatitis. This particular disease could mean he could be dead by his third birthday, they told me, and he could put other lives at risk. They were pretty sure the American immigration authorities wouldn't let him in the country. The orphanage officials said they'd redo the test, but I could barely

---

[7]Amy Laura Hall, *Conceiving Parenthood: American Protestantism and the Spirit of Reproduction* (Grand Rapids, MI: Eerdmans, 2008), 394.

hear them. I was nauseated with grief. It felt like another miscarriage, but this time of a child whose face I'd seen, whose little body I'd hugged.

That night Maria and I went back to the home we were staying in, in the city. I did something I'm embarrassed to say I'd never done before, but something my Lord did often—I prayed all night. I happened to be reading through Genesis at that time, and that very day I had read of Joseph sending his brothers back from Egypt to retrieve their younger brother Benjamin. In the narrative, Jacob didn't want to let Benjamin go. I could resonate with the anguish in his voice as he cried out, "And as for me, if I am bereaved of my children, I am bereaved" (43:14). I cried out to God for mercy, for this child's life. I hadn't wanted a child with a disease—certainly not one with a life-threatening, dangerous disease—but I wanted him. I'd grown in just a few days' time to love him, and it somehow now seemed worth it, whatever the risk. I was already mapping out a game plan involving my old boss (a U.S. Congressman) and every other contact I might have to get this child into the country.

After a night of fasting, praying, and crying, I walked into the kitchen to see Maria standing with our translator. He was reporting that the new blood test revealed no traces of any disease. My knees buckled as my spirit within me seemed to cry out with thanksgiving like I'd never experienced before.

Maria and I had planned to name this child Andrew Fuller Moore after a great nineteenth-century Baptist preacher, one of the sparks of the modern missions movement. I turned to her and said, "His name is Benjamin. Benjamin Jacob Moore."

There turned out to be nothing "wrong" with Benjamin (or with his brother Timothy), at least not long-term. There would have been nothing heroic about our caring for him if there was. He was our son, and that's what you do when you love someone.

Sure, there's a risk for you if you adopt. Sure, your child may turn out to have problems you can't foresee, and you may wonder how you could bear it, especially if you've already been through the grief of infertility or the death of children. But if that does happen, you won't be dealing with autism or cancer or cerebral palsy or AIDS as "things." You'll be caring for your child.

And, again, there are scarier risks than disease or disability, especially for those of us who know Jesus. We know what the world doesn't acknowledge, that all of us are terminally ill a sickness cured only through resurrection. None of us is guaranteed that our children will join us in this narrow path toward the kingdom. That's what keeps me awake at night now, not wondering about family medical histories. I pray now that little Benjamin will live up to his namesake.

Benjamin, after all, didn't return home to Jacob because of his own power. His brother Judah guaranteed his return. Judah said to old Israel, "I will be a pledge of his safety. From my hand you shall require him" (Gen. 43:9). Benjamin was "a ravenous wolf," Jacob said, "dividing the spoil" (Gen. 49:27), but his prowess couldn't save him. Only the tribe of Judah could do that, a tribe that brought forth to us its final son, our Lord Jesus. We want the house of Benjamin to decrease in our son's life, and the house of Judah to increase.

Who knows what the future holds for my sons—or for whatever children the Lord may call you or your loved ones to adopt? The question is, do you trust Jesus, with their stories and with yours?

CONCLUSION

It's true that adoption isn't "natural." We have adoptions because we live in a world groaning under the curse of sin and death. Fathers abandon mothers. Mothers get pregnant without marriage. Parents are killed. Diseases ravage villages. It was not so from the beginning. The hard questions about adoption—and the easy ones too—are only with us because something's gone wrong with the world.

Adoption is modeled after the natural family. But the biological family is also modeled after something—the kingdom of God in Christ. King Jesus tells us his reign is hidden from "the wise and understanding" but is revealed to "little children" (Matt. 11:25).

The childlike kingdom we've come into is filled with transracial adoptees like you and me. It's made up of "special-needs" orphans like us. Sometimes adoptions turn out with families that look remarkably similar—almost "natural," you might say. But let's not fall for the carnality that values boys over girls, that pits ethnicities against one another, or that is repulsed by physical or emotional weakness. Let's be the people of Christ, and, like him, let's teach ourselves to welcome children into our homes, even those our culture tells us we're not supposed to want.

7

It Takes a Village to Adopt a Child

How Churches Can Encourage Adoption

IT STILL HAD THAT SMELL, like a mixture of new carpet and old lady. Maria and I looked at each other as we stood in this familiar foyer. It was the first place we'd ever seen each other—as I ran in from the rain and she was folding up a drenched umbrella. I'd walked in this door thousands of times. My parents carried me in these doors a few weeks after my birth. I'd walked through them every Sunday morning of my childhood, with a Bible and an offering envelope in hand. Every summer I marched through these doors— carrying a flag or a Bible for the round of Vacation Bible School pledges, the closest things we had to a liturgy or a calendar of the Christian year. I looked at the window, right next to the big glass doors. That was the one the preacher's son had smashed with a rock, and we'd all scattered, knowing he was going to get it. This was my home church. It'd been a long time since we'd walked into this foyer, and now we had two little hands gripping our fingers.

Our boys had, I'm sure, no idea how big a deal it was for us to have them here with us. To them, it was just another church some-where. But to me it was everything. And to them, though they'll probably never know it, it will mean everything. Because I sit down every night and read the Bible to them. I first learned to believe the Bible here, in this church. I pray at the dinner table every night. It was at this church where I first learned to pray. It was from these people standing over offering plates or sick lists where I first heard prayers. Our sons often say the words "Mom" and "Dad," but those names wouldn't apply to Maria and me—together—if we hadn't found each other here. They go to church every Sunday, and these people taught me to want to have a church to come home to. In a very real sense, my boys are being reared by the church in which we are now members but also by a church of people they'd never recognize.

For those of us who follow Jesus, this is true of all of us, whether we see it or not. In saying that this chapter is about how the church can encourage adoption, I'm afraid of being misunderstood, given the lack of attention to the church in contemporary American Christianity.

I'm afraid some people will think I'm referring to the church generically as a synonym for Christians, some invisible blob of everyone who believes the same facts about a Galilean or who follows the same principles from the first century. In the New Testament, though, the church is something more concrete than that. Yes, the church is that transnational, trans-generational Body of Christ, the redeemed of all of the ages. But the church expresses itself in this age in local, palpable gatherings of believers in covenant with one another. When I say "church," I'm speaking largely of how we live our lives together in these little outposts of the kingdom of Christ.

I'm afraid some people will think I'm referring to the church programmatically as a set of initiatives. In the case of adoption, some of the need is for programs and strategies. But far more important than more "special emphases" is a culture of bringing Christ's presence to orphans. This has to do with creating a culture of adoption. In many ways, this is carried through more in thousands of conversations in hallways, fellowship dinners around a common table, and gospel preaching than in new initiatives and curricula and plans.

Most importantly, we must recognize that adoption isn't an issue for individual Christian families. There's no such thing as a "Christian family" abstracted from the church. It also is not simply an issue for an interest group within the church—the "adoption people" competing with the "homeschooling people" competing with the "Third World debt relief people" and so on. Adoption can be a priority for everyone within the church in ways that reflect the diversity and unity of a church that is one body with many members. Adoption can be part of our congregational lives, fully recognizing the differing gifts and callings of individual Christians within the church.

If adoption is to be a priority for us, we must transform the local community—the internal ministry of the church—and the global vision—the external witness of the church. In this way, our churches can work together with other like-minded congregations toward a witness that is expansively pro-life, pro-family, pro-orphan, and pro-gospel.

ADOPTION AND THE LOCAL VISION OF THE CHURCH

For most churches, adoption isn't a priority, and this isn't because the church members are anti-adoption. It's because adoption seems strange to some of them and irrelevant to others. It becomes a focus only when a church member personally faces infertility or knows of particular children without parents. Until then, for most of us, adoption rarely crosses our minds.

That's why the first step to being an adoption-friendly church must be the pulpit. That seems obvious, but it's less obvious than it seems. By saying that pastors should preach on adoption, I am not speaking primarily of raising awareness about adoption, in the same way a high school principal can raise awareness in a speech about a fund-raising drive for the new football stadium. Preaching isn't simply conveying information.

Within the church, preaching is a profoundly spiritual reality in which the preacher stands in the place of Christ as an ambassador delivering a word on behalf of the ruler (2 Cor. 5:18–20). When the preacher brings to the people an accurate and passionate rendering of the Word of God, the Spirit of Jesus is there, applying the Word to the hearers. The act of preaching then carries with it, if it is biblically faithful gospel preaching, the authority of Jesus himself. That's the difference between the act of preaching and the act of lecture delivery—the difference between "Thus saith the Lord" and "It seems to me."

Because God creates via words (Jer. 51:15–16), he uses preaching to call into existence spiritual realities that didn't exist before (Ezek. 37:4). The very act of preaching makes things happen; it forces a confrontation not just between people and ideas, but also between people and the Spirit. A pastor's preaching on the cosmic and missional aspects of adoption will not come back void. It will create a reality within the church, wherever there are those who are willing to hear the voice of Christ, who don't harden their hearts but listen in belief (Heb. 3:7–4:16).

For churches to see adoption as a priority means that pastors must speak not simply to the will or to the mind or to the sentiments but to the moral imagination. The pastor must allow his people to see the goodness and glory of adoption as an icon of the gospel they embrace. He can do so by preaching with the kind of passion that forces his people to "see" with their hearts the kind of possibilities he's holding forth. Whenever earthly things mirror heavenly realities, a preacher is needed to point from the picture to the thing pictured, showing us why we should love both.

The preacher, moreover, should preach on adoption with specificity. The pastor doesn't know exactly how an adoption priority works itself out in each individual life or family, but he can further the cause by provoking questions. He can ask, for instance, in a message on poverty or the sanctity of human life, whether God might be calling some in the congregation that day to adopt or to give money to fund an adoption. He can call on his people to pray about how God would have them serve the fatherless, giving information on how they can carry out whatever commitment God lays on their hearts, providing contact information about groups within the church that are able to help.

One area of needed reformation in our preaching is in wedding sermons. Too many of our weddings, even in the most conservative churches, pretend as though the event is about the formation of a "couple." The language of older wedding ceremonies, which mention procreation and the children of the union, seem quaint and antiquarian to our ears. We're the ones who are odd, however, not our forebears. Marriage is about the formation of a new family. What would happen if our wedding ceremonies were less about a "celebration of the love of Joni and Todd" and more about the formation of a new covenant family? What if the officiating pastor spoke to the couple not only about what it means to be a faithful husband and wife but what it will mean to be a faithful father and mother? What if every wedding ceremony included a prayer for the children of the union, that such children might actually be and that they'd be saved at an early age? What if this prayer included the mention of such children as coming either through birth or through adoption? Such small measures could help refocus our minds and hearts on our responsibilities to the next generation.

Pastors and church leaders can also create a priority for adoption by highlighting adoptions within the church. This isn't a way to commend the adopting parents but rather to make adoption seem less strange to the rest of the congregation. In almost any given church service, there are those who will start to think about whether they should adopt if they just see someone who has done it. When people see and know children who've been adopted, suddenly the reality isn't abstract to them. When they hear the word *orphan*, they stop thinking of a sad face in a movie and start thinking of Caleb or Chloe who sits in the pew in front of them.

If your church has Bible study groups or discipleship cells, these smaller groups can get involved in the adoption process right along with the adopting family. For most adopting families, "arrival day" is every bit the flurry of activity as going into labor—and sometimes even more sudden. The small group can have folks signed up to pray and fast through the days and nights leading up to adoption, especially if there are questions about whether a birth mother might change her mind or whether an adoption might fall through in some other way. The group can provide meals for the family in the days and weeks ahead as the adopting parents adjust to the child's arrival in the home. They might provide childcare for any brothers or sisters already part of the family, maybe even plan special activities for them—like trips to the zoo—as they adjust to the new reality in their house. Adopting parents sometimes feel lonely and scared in the process. Walking off an airplane or stepping into their front yard after a drive from the hospital to find their fellow Christians holding signs with confetti flying in celebration can be a great encouragement to the parents. It can also help highlight adoption to others within the congregation by making them part of a family's pilgrimage.

Some churches have a time of "baby dedication" or "parent and child dedication" in which they pray for new arrivals within the congregation. Some congregations are of such a massive size that a once-a-year celebration is all that's practical. For other churches, though, there could be a time at the end of the service whenever a baby is born or a child is adopted by a family within the church. This could take as little as three or four minutes with recognition and a prayer of thanksgiving. In larger churches, this could even be done via video. The point would be to counter the culture's growing utilitarian view of children, to welcome children as blessings from God, and to encourage families to consider adopting orphans into their homes.

A pastor-hero of mine used to conclude every baptism by standing in the baptistery, dipping his hands in the water, and announcing, "And yet there is room for more." It was his way of inviting those listening to come into the fellowship of Christ without delay. A pastor could have great effect if he held a time of prayer for adopting families, followed by the statement to his people, "And yet there are more children out there who need godly parents."

Once children are seen as a blessing, and once adoption doesn't seem strange or exotic, an adoption culture tends to flourish in gospel-anchored churches. This is why you rarely see in healthy churches just one or two couples with children who've been adopted. Once a family or two adopts, there tends to be a flurry of adoptions.

Mother's Day is a particularly sensitive time in most congregations, and many pastors and church leaders don't even know it. Infertile women often find this day almost unbearable, not because they're bitter or covetous or envious, but simply because it's a reminder of unfulfilled longings. Some pastors, commendably, mention in their sermons and prayers on this day those who would love to be parents but haven't yet been given this opportunity.

What if, though, pastors and church leaders were to set aside a day for prayer for children for the infertile? In too many churches, ministry to infertile couples is relegated to support groups that meet in the church basement during the week, under cover of darkness. It's true that infertile couples need each other, and the time of prayer and counsel with people in similar circumstances can be helpful. But this alone can contribute to the sense of isolation and even shame experienced by those hurting in this way. What if, at the end of the service, the pastor called any person or couple who wanted prayer for children to come forward and then asked others in the congregation to gather around them and pray? Not every person grappling with infertility will do this publicly, but many will. And even those too embarrassed or private to come forward will be encouraged by a church willing to pray for those hurting in this way. The pastor could pray for God's gift of children for these couples, either through biological procreation or through adoption, whichever the Lord desires in each case.

Another key aspect of local church ministry toward adoption is that of economic stewardship. If the apostles reminded even Paul himself to "remember the poor" (Gal. 2:10), then surely the rest of us need such a reminder. The problem is, again, we just don't see how to do so. There are often within any given congregation older individuals or couples who aren't able or called to adopt but who have the means to equip a younger, economically struggling family to do so. If churches appealed to such persons to consider whether they could help fund an adoption, a vast army of such believers would do so.

The pastor could stand up and say, "We have an unnamed couple in our congregation that's praying for the money it will take to adopt a child. I wonder if the Lord's calling anyone here to help make this happen." Churches can further this along by allowing givers to do so anonymously, knowing they'll be rewarded in full at the Judgment Seat of Christ.

Some Christians aren't able to give money toward adoption, but they might be able to give low-interest loans to a couple seeking to adopt. If this were mentioned as a possible route to ministry to the fatherless, some would stand up to do it, especially those whose lives or families have been affected by adoption.

God has blessed some churches with relatively large sums of money. Many congregations may find it to be the Father's will to forgo the new Family Life Center in order to help establish some families, to save some lives. A church probably wouldn't want to establish a wide-open giveaway of money to people seeking to adopt, regardless of who is asking. Such a policy would likely overwhelm a church and put someone in the awkward situation of sorting through questions that the church is not quite prepared to answer. What do you do when a Unitarian couple from the community asks for help adopting? What do you do when a single woman down the street asks for such assistance? What do you do when the "power couple" earning a quarter of a million dollars a year seeks help?

Some of these situations can be avoided by restricting assistance to church members, those under the discipline and care of the church. The church might seek to give the money as matching funds, supplementing money earned elsewhere by a family in order to spread out the resources to more families within the congregation. Other churches may offer grants to pay for specific aspects of the adoption—say, the overseas portion or the home study aspect of adoption expenses. Again, rarely would these funds have to come largely from the church's general budget. There are Christians everywhere—including, most likely, in your church or community—who would give specifically to this, over and above their tithes and offerings.

The possibilities are wide-open for economically empowering families to adopt. These are just a few of them. A congregation that embraces the priority of adoption will find all sorts of ways to help those who want to adopt—from attorneys granting their expertise *pro bono* to restaurants setting aside part of their earnings on a given day to promote adoption and so forth.

The congregation can also work to help with the logistical legwork of an adoption. The congregation I serve provides for church members a list of adoption agencies and home study specialists that members of the church have used, along with information about whether these agencies work domestically or internationally and, if the latter, the countries in which they operate. The church also provides ballpark figures of costs associated with each kind of adoption. It is important, though, that if your church does this, you encourage prospective parents to talk with those who've adopted through these agencies and services, noting that your congregation does not necessarily endorse any particular agency. This will protect your church from any unexpected change in direction of a given agency and will encourage prospective parents to check out the terrain in front of them thoroughly.

More important than any particular initiative for adoption is the need to create a vision of the church as a household. A major stumbling block to adoption, as we've seen, is our inherent carnality. One adoption expert writes that adoption confuses contemporary culture because we can't decide whether the adoptive family is "as if begotten" or if blood kinship is really what matters.[1] The answer to this, of course, is the church, an entity that transcends both blood kinship and legal fictions.

In most conservative churches, we rightly emphasize the impor-

---

[1]Barbara Melosh, *Strangers and Kin: The American Way of Adoption* (Cambridge, MA: Harvard University Press, 2002), 290.

tance of the family. Sometimes, though, we act as though the church exists simply to help equip the family to be the family. Sometimes pastors will preach that the family precedes both the church and the state, thinking this will prove the family's preeminence over both of these other institutions. This statement isn't really true, though. The family does, of course, precede and is more important than provisional human governments. The original family of Eden, though, was both a family and a "church"—that is, an assembly of those in covenant with God and to each other, designed to worship him and to carry out his mission on the earth.

Marriage is important because it's about more than simply a sexual or companionate union; it points to the mystery of Christ and his church (Eph. 5:22–33). In the same way, the family is highly important, partly because of the way it points to the church as "the household of God" (1 Tim. 3:15). We cannot then focus on our families without a focus on the church. Adoption will never be a priority for our churches until our churches see how our adoption—together—has formed a new family.

One key way for this to happen is for pastors and church leaders to recover the role of spiritual fathers and mothers within the church, an image found throughout the New Testament (e.g., 1 Cor. 4:15). In a world in which so many of our younger generation limps along, wounded by father-absence, what would happen if pastors modeled the loving authority of fathers in their churches? What if more of our young men and women looked with respect and love to their spiritual fathers as real pastors in real congregations rather than to cardboard celebrities hawking products from television screens or the shelves of Christian bookstores? What if we recovered the glory of spiritual mothers within the church—older women who nurture and train the generations of younger women following them (Titus 2:3–5)?

Too often, our concept of pastors and church leaders reinforces rather than obliterates the sad state of family life in our current context. When pastors are distant and impersonal or when they replace their authority as a man of God with a breezy casualness, they miss the opportunity to model the church as household.

Pastors, proclaim the fatherhood of God and concretize in your preaching what this fatherhood looks like. Our churches often don't "get" adoption, first and foremost, because they don't "get" God. Yes, we're right to warn our people away from a "Jesus is my buddy" type of familiarity with the Almighty, emphasizing instead the glory and awe and holiness and otherness of God. Sometimes, though, in our zeal to do this, we neglect the nearness of our God, our beholding his glory in the flesh of our Brother-Lord. Preach the glory of God, but preach the glory the way he reveals it—in Jesus Christ. Remind your people of God's love and acceptance of them, his ongoing provision for them in Christ.

In your preaching, pastors, announce that the church is a new family, and specify how the members of the Body are to love one another in that way. The apostle Paul looked for specific examples of bearing with one another—eating only vegetables or meat, for instance (Rom. 14)—and pastors can do the same in their preaching. A pastor might, for instance, point out the fact that some members of the congregation are avid hunters with National Rifle Association bumper stickers on their trucks, while other members of the congregation are animal protection enthusiasts who believe shooting a defenseless deer is Neanderthal. The pastor might point out that these differences don't divide people in this congregation, because we're brothers and sisters.

In some churches, some doctrinal issues aren't on the level of barriers to Christian fellowship but are nevertheless highly controversial. What if a pastor, while preaching on, say, the timing of the Rapture in relation to the Great Tribulation or the relationship of predestination to human freedom, pointed out someone in the congregation who holds the opposite view in order to say, "She and I don't see on this issue eye-to-eye, but we learn from each other and love each other because we're family"? There are, of course, issues essential to the faith and to the mission of a church that the church shouldn't compromise on at all. A church that bears with a non-Trinitarian member isn't loving but licentious. Moreover, there are aspects of the church's task on which there must be agreement in order to carry out that task together. A church has to agree, for example, on who to baptize and how, who to ordain and by what authority, and so forth. There are many, many other issues, however, in which we don't have agreement, but we, in the words of the apostle Paul, disagree as brothers, not enemies (2 Thess. 3:13–15).

Our concept of the church as household necessarily entails a recovery of the meaning of the Lord's Table in many of our churches. The Supper that Jesus gave us is itself a living sign of adoption. Table fellowship, after all, is a familial activity. This is why Jesus was so revolutionary when he announced, "Many will come from east and west and recline at table with Abraham, Isaac, and Jacob in the kingdom of heaven" (Matt. 8:11). Why do our Lord's Supper services so often look like the clinical, communal rinse-and-spit of fluoride at an elementary school than like a loving family gathered around a feast table?

Often I'll preach in churches about the Lord's Supper and will call on congregations to go back to using a common loaf and a common cup, with the bread being torn, not daintily picked up in prefabricated bits, and with each person drinking the wine and passing the cup along. I don't mind folks disagreeing with me on this. I'm just stunned by the reason they most often give for dismissing this ancient Christian practice: germs. The common cup is, well, gross to many Christians because they don't like the idea of drinking after strangers. That's just the point, though. You're not drinking after strangers. You're drinking after your own flesh and blood, your family.

An adoption culture cannot flourish without a sense of meaningful church membership. If you can't distinguish between siblings and strangers in your own fellowship, don't expect families to be able to do so in their own homes. Sometimes Christians, especially those of the World War II and baby-boomer generations, tend to think that church discipline is counter-evangelistic. Doesn't it do people good to be members of churches, even if they never attend? No. It's actually just the opposite. When you affirm as members people you don't expect to see in the kingdom of God, you're signaling to the community that you don't really believe what you say you believe. If you don't love your alleged brother or sister enough to warn him or her of possible damnation, then how do you expect families, adopting or otherwise, to understand the permanence and perseverance it takes to love each other to the very end?

The recovery of the church as household is furthermore seen in the way the church uses the spiritual gifts. In too many of our congregations, spiritual gifts are seen through a hyper-individualist grid. We tell our people how to "unwrap" their gifts, to take a personality profile to find out what their gift is. We say, "Every member is a minister," but what we typically mean is, "Every member should serve on a committee." The gifts in the New Testament, though, function as part of a home economy as the household is built up through the various parts thereof. In the New Testament we don't find our gift through self-examination and introspection and then find ways to express it. Instead we love one another, serve one another, help one another, and in so doing we see how God has equipped us to do so. This is why Paul always speaks of the spiritual gifts in terms of the whole body, of order, and of the primacy of love (1 Cor. 12–14).

The way we see such things has everything to do with the way we see our family responsibilities, including the joy of adoption. Speaking of the family, Wendell Berry laments the fact that so many crucial aspects of familial life have been outsourced to corporations through such means as institutionalized day care, preschool, and nursing homes. Berry notes:

> A family necessarily begins to come apart if it gives its children entirely to the care of the school or the police, and its old people entirely to the care of the health industry. Nobody can deny the value of good care even away from home to people who have become helplessly ill or crippled or, in our present circumstances,

the value of good daytime care for the children of single parents who have to work. Nevertheless, it is the purpose of the family to stay together. And like a community, a family doesn't just stay together out of sentiment. It is certainly more apt to stay together if the various members need one another or are in some practical way dependent on one another. It's probably worth the risk to say that families need to have useful work for their children and old people, little jobs that the other members are glad to have done.[2]

Isn't this precisely what God has given us in the church? He's given us a household in which even the seemingly least significant member is part of the family's common purpose, doing his or her part in the life of the household. Could it be that we value corporate success and youthful vitality in our homes because this is what we learn to value in our churches?

If your local church starts to take on the spiritual marks of a family, a true kinship group brought together in Christ, you'll know it. You'll begin to see people praying for one another, hugging one another, kissing one another, looking out for one another's interests above their own. When our churches are countercultural kingdom outposts, we'll start to see the joy of a life that's more meaningful than a two-car garage and a vacation at this year's faddish theme park. Once people learn to see their brothers and sisters and fathers and mothers in ways more significant than simply the flesh, adoption just doesn't seem so strange anymore.

ADOPTION AND THE GLOBAL VISION OF THE CHURCH

On both of our trips to Russia, Maria and I found ourselves staying in a home rented out by our agency for families adopting from the region. The house was small, and we weren't permitted to leave except to walk around the neighborhood and make our daily trips to the orphanage. In such circumstances, we got to know our house-

---

[2]Holly M. Brockman, "Wendell Berry's Thoughts on the Good Life," *New Southerner: An Anthology, 2005-2006*, 9–13.

mates quite well. We were the only Christians in the house, on both trips. At one point, as I watched an adopting couple scream at one another across the table, I looked over at Maria with raised eyebrows as if to say, "These people made it through a home study?" The more I thought about it, though, the more I was convicted about my condemnatory attitude. What I couldn't shake was the question, where are all the Christians?

I know our situation was probably unique. There are Christians, after all, adopting in large numbers. Even so, why isn't adoption an emphasis as a Great Commission priority for more of our churches? Adoption is, after all, evangelistic to the core. When a Christian family adopts a child, that family is committing to years of gospel proclamation, of seeking to see this child come to faith in Christ. There are several ways churches can include adoption in their global vision for world missions.

The first is, simply, to recognize adoption as an aspect of Christian mission. That, again, starts in the pulpit. Just as you would call your people to consider the plight of children starving around the world, plead with them to consider the plight of children without parents in your neighborhood and across the oceans. Recognize the spiritual warfare aspects of this, as we've previously discussed in this book, and call your people, particularly your men, to engage in this warfare. Too often we assume adoption is a "women's issue." Call your men to their roles as protectors and providers for children who aren't their own, yet.

There are other ways, though, beyond the preaching ministry, to signal adoption as part of the church's mission agenda. The church I now serve as a preaching pastor has for years sought to keep a Great Commission focus constantly before the attention of the people. In the foyer of the church are wall-to-ceiling world maps with pictures of missionaries from the church next to the countries or regions in which they serve. The church wisely (and this was done years before I ever arrived, so I claim no credit for it) also includes a world map with pictures of families who've adopted next to the state, country, or region from which they adopted. This simple gesture signals to the congregation that adoption is a Great Commission activity.

At the same time, children who've been adopted can reinforce the bigger issue of global missions. Parents who've adopted a child from the mountains of eastern Kentucky or from the city streets of Philadelphia are going to have a particular burden for the people of those regions and are quite likely to bring attention to the pressing need there. Parents who've adopted from Russia are perfect candidates to lead a mission trip to that area of the former Soviet Union. Parents who have adopted from China are more likely to lead a prayer ministry for the persecuted church there. As a pastor calls his congregation to a vision for the nations, he can point to children within that congregation who have come from backgrounds all over the country and the world, pressing his congregation to evangelize their kinsmen according to the flesh. The children running through your church halls can be a perpetual signal to pray and labor for the nations to know Christ.

A largely untilled field for local church evangelism is that of non-Christian families in the adoption process. Your church could partner with adoption agencies in your community to offer seminars and adoption fairs in your church, say, on a Friday night or a Saturday afternoon. Your congregation could offer information at the seminar about free parenting classes for adopting couples. Many of these families will want to connect with others who've adopted. If you have such families in your church, you can offer one-on-one counsel for adopting families. This will give you the opportunity to get to know families you may never otherwise meet. Moreover, these families are often thinking about adoption-specific questions at this time. Can I love someone who's not blood-related to me? What does the future hold for me and for my child? How much of my child's identity is already in her genes? These questions, as we've seen, ultimately point to eternal matters. You know why they're so important because you know what it means to find adoption in Christ. Through these ministries, you may find children being adopted on the earthly plane and parents being adopted in the heavenly plane.

It's important not to give the impression that your church is open only to those adopting families who "have it all together." Church membership is for the repentant, of course, but the gospel is for everyone. Welcome into such ministries those you might not believe ought to adopt at all—the cohabiting couple, the thrice-married single mother, the unmarried prescription drug addict, and so forth.

Your congregation could also provide ministries to those sometimes forgotten in the adoption process. You could have a small group for ministry to women who've placed their babies up for adoption. Again, a relationship with one or more adoption agencies or social workers in your community could facilitate this, as many would like to have such options available to tell birth mothers about as they move through the process. Your church could have classes for grandparents in adopting families, led by grandparents in your church. Sometimes extended family members don't know how they should respond to an adoption since they've never seen one up close before. Again, this could provide opportunities to connect with people who ordinarily might not see the relevance of your church to their lives.

Local congregations also can include adoption as part of their witness to Christ by ministering to women and children in crisis. The need for adoption in our context is rarely because of death. It is far more typically the result of an absent or abusive father, children conceived without the stability of marriage, and resulting economic and social horrors. Moreover, one of the reasons domestic adoption is increasingly difficult is not because children who need to be adopted don't exist. It's instead because many of them are snuffed out in the womb. In post-*Roe v. Wade* America, many women (mistakenly) believe that aborting will be less emotionally traumatic for them than seeing their children adopted into new families, a perception that the abortion industry and its propagandists are more than willing to reinforce. Mother Theresa famously pleaded with any pregnant women within the sound of her voice to give her their babies if they didn't want them, and she would raise them. Perhaps more of our congregations should say the same thing.

In your community, churches could cooperate together to sponsor centers for pregnant women in crisis, sometimes right near abortion clinics. Your congregation or group of congregations could provide pregnancy tests, ultrasounds, and counseling to pregnant women, along with a commitment to find adopting parents for those who choose not to abort. Think of the opportunities from such an endeavor to share Christ, both with mothers and, ultimately, with children.

Moreover, think of the public witness for Christ your church could have simply by making clear that you, like your Lord Jesus, care about widows and orphans, whatever their situation. Many single mothers, for instance, are able to raise their children but must work—sometimes two or three jobs—in order to provide for them. Often churches have day-care centers, and often these centers are financially beneficial to the church. Too often these centers are less about ministry to the community than about providing a service to upwardly mobile, dual-income families. It could be, though, that the Lord is calling your church to provide childcare, along with a strong emphasis on Christian evangelism and discipleship, to the children of these desperate mothers in your community, and to do it for little or no cost to them.

In the past century, many orphanages and children's homes were church-based, founded and funded by Christian denominations or groups. Some of these are still doing much-needed kingdom work. There are far too few of them, though. Like Christian colleges and universities, some of these agencies have a Christian heritage but no distinctly Christian identity. Because they take state money, they must follow state regulations and thus, in some places, aren't able to have evangelism as the explicit purpose of their adoption and foster care programs. But these agencies are still doing worthy service. In many of our denominations in the United States, we have the means to fund more orphanages and children's homes with an explicitly Great Commission purpose, seeking to find strongly Christian homes for children. Often birth mothers, even unbelievers, feel more comfortable having their children grow up in Christian homes. Being able to point to a multitude of ministries that can make this happen quickly and effectively would be an advance for the cause of Christ.

The same is true with international adoption as it relates to global missions. Most local churches cooperate with other churches, through denominations or parachurch ministries, for international missionary activity. Few missionary agencies, though, incorporate international adoption into their strategies.

What if, though, some mission agencies planted outposts near strategic orphanages around the world, providing housing and ministry opportunities for adopting Christian families? Prospective parents sometimes wait to adopt for weeks overseas. For some of them, there could be coordinated opportunities to minister to the orphans and people in the community. For others, there could be homes for adopting parents that could function as discipleship centers, training parents to raise their new children in ways consonant with the gospel. Mission agencies could evangelize unbelieving adopting parents, many of whom are thinking about ultimate things for the first time in a long while as they face a time of life transition.

This missional witness through care for orphans also could transform Christian influence in the public square. Christian churches have, from the beginning, stood against abortion and infanticide. Too often, though, the culture around us mistakenly believes this stance is punitive, even misogynist. We oppose abortion, our neighbors sometimes assume, because we wish to punish women for having sex.

United States Congressman Barney Frank, an abortion rights supporter, famously quipped that pro-lifers believe that "life begins at conception and ends at birth." This quote is cited often, usually as a distraction, as though caring for children must necessarily entail a consensus on how the national government should provide for nutrition, health care, and so forth. Still, the staying power of the statement shows how those on the outside sometimes perceive Christian commitment to life. Of course, to a large degree Christians will not be able to convince hard-core ideologues on this and similar issues, regardless of what actions they take or don't take. Some who support abortion rights the strongest take a dim view of adoption. Churches known for equipping believers to adopt, however, can at least start to counter misconceived perceptions by showing a pro-life witness that is as obviously love-oriented as it is truth-oriented.

As the church teaches its people to care for the fatherless, the more will Christians within the Body exercise their Romans 13 responsibility as members of a democratic republic (and thus part of the powers that be) to redirect the sword of the state away from the innocent unborn. As they do this, those with influence in public policy can seek to find ways to make adoption easier and more affordable, while at the same time keeping adoption safe and just for birth mothers, children, and adopting families.

The primary means of furthering adoption as mission, though, may seemingly have little to do with adoption at all. The most important aspect of creating an adoption culture is preaching the gospel.

Pastors can encourage adoption also as they continually emphasize the sanctity of human life, including the lives of the disabled, the "illegitimate," and the unborn. In any given service, the pastor will be preaching to some who are now facing or one day will face the temptation to extinguish the life of a child. Yes, it is commendable that pastors are willing to denounce abortion as a social and personal evil. Some of our people conclude, though, that the answer is simply to vote for the "right" candidates for public office.

Some of the women in your congregation are vulnerable to the abortionists' propaganda precisely because they feel they'll lose their church if church people know about the shame of their pregnancy. Speak to such a woman from the pulpit, and to her husband or boyfriend or father. Speak directly to the abortionist who may have slipped in the back door or may come across a recording of the message. Speak directly of the horror of the judgment to come for those who shed innocent blood. But proclaim just as openly that judgment has fallen on the quivering body of a crucified Jesus. Warn of hell, but offer mercy—mercy not only at the Judgment Seat but mercy in the cell groups and hallways of your church.

The unbelievers in your community—or in the mission fields you serve around the world—are hungering for belonging. You know this. Show them, then, the beauty of what the Scripture says about adoption in Christ. Whether in your one-on-one witnessing or in your pulpit proclamation, unpack the glory of this cosmic adoption and show how this adoption is pictured in flesh-and-blood adopting situations in your own congregation. Plead with sinners to embrace their Father, to find a new family.

CONCLUSION

Several years ago, the "culture wars" in America boiled down to a single African proverb. The saying—employed by, among others, a controversial First Lady of the United States—was, "It takes a village to raise a child." Traditionalists countered this saying with a rejoinder: "No, it takes a family to raise a child." The conservatives were right, of course—at least inasmuch as the "village" referred to by some equaled the impersonal bureaucracies of the state.

In another sense, though, the African proverb is strikingly biblical. No child is to grow up simply within the confines of his family. No individual believer is discipled alone. We're created to be brought "to mature manhood, to the measure of the stature of the fullness of Christ" (Eph. 4:13) through the church. We're ecclesially formed in every way, including in our lives as members of biologically or adoptively formed families. That's why passages on the responsibilities of parents and children are written not simply to the parties involved but to entire congregations (e.g., Eph. 6:1–4).

Through our life within the Body of Christ, we grow to resemble Jesus, together. This resemblance then transforms our local communion and our global mission. The Bible's call to protect the widow and the fatherless is written to no one individual—and certainly not to Caesar's government—but "to the twelve tribes in the Dispersion" (James 1:1). What we need, then, is a congregational counterculture, at the local level, and a congregational counter-vision, at the global level.

One day my children will, if the Lord wills, have children of their own. Their children will ask them, "Where did you come from?" That'll be a more complicated question for them than it would be for most of their peers. I hope they're able to take them back to the orphanage—if they can find it—in rural Russia.

But I hope also they take them to the church building here in Louisville where they learned to see the gospel in visual form. And I hope, if they get the chance, that they'll take those children to see a little red brick church in coastal Mississippi. They don't know a soul there, but that church helped raise them too.

Your congregation can encourage and equip the adoption of infants and children. Your church can preach the gospel and care for the vulnerable. You can provide the funds and the encouragement and the prayer support for untold numbers of Great Commission families. If adoption is to be a priority, it will take mobilizing congregations to do so. After all, it takes more than a village to adopt a child, at least for those of us in Christ. It takes a church.

8

Adopted Is a Past-Tense Verb

*How Parents, Children, and Friends Can Think about
Growing up Adopted*

IF YOU WANT TO UNDERSTAND American culture, watch
an episode or two of *The Brady Bunch*. That's the conclusion of envi-
ronmentalist Bill McKibben, who notes that one large demographic
segment of Americans know *The Brady Bunch* television program
better than their own parents' birthdays. McKibben contends that
the program showcases the artificiality of contemporary suburban
American life, "a life where no work is done—usually not even by
the maid—because there are appliances in every corner." Perhaps
most artificial and American is the very thesis of the show: this group
had somehow formed a family, and that's the way they all became
the Brady Bunch. "But this never caused any tension in the show,"
McKibben writes.[1]

He's on to something here, when you think about it. Mike Brady
instantly became "Dad," and Carol immediately was "Mom." The
brothers and the sisters were siblings as soon as the wedding vows
were pronounced. Yes, there were struggles in the house. Jan envied
Marcia, but she never displayed a crush on Greg. Mike Brady offered
calm, fatherly advice at the end of the day, but he never heard Marcia
screaming back at him, "You're not my real dad! I don't have to
listen to you!" The family vacation might be disrupted by a curse on
a Hawaiian idol statuette, but not by Mike yelling at Carol, "I don't
care if they do have hair of gold, your girls are driving me crazy. The

---

[1] Bill McKibben, "What's On: 11:30 A.M.," in *The Bill McKibben Reader: Pieces from an Active Life*
(New York: Holt, 2008), 101.

middle one is clearly nuts, and get the youngest one in speech therapy already. I don't care if she is only 'theven.'"

The Brady Bunch, like the more typically nuclear family sitcoms that preceded it, was built around a picture of "normal." The point was to make the viewer think, "I wish I had a family like that. Then we'd be like everyone else." But this wasn't and isn't normal. These televised families were, in the words of one marriage scholar "the way we never were."[2]

In a post-Fall world, being part of a family is tough, regardless of the circumstances. The stakes are much bigger than the kinds of mild screen-written crises that can be resolved in a twenty-two minute script. Adoption complicates that already complicated reality even further. Whether you're a potentially adopting parent, a parent who has adopted children already, someone who was adopted yourself, or someone with a burden for adoption in your church or community, you need to be aware of some common struggles that come along with growing up after adoption. Like the event of adoption itself, these struggles can, if we have ears to hear and eyes to see, point us to the gospel that saves us.

BELONGING AND ACCEPTANCE

It's a bird. It's a plane. It's a Soviet agent. Several years ago, a comic book artist re-imagined the Superman myth with a graphic novel about the son of Krypton landing in 1930s Ukraine instead of Smallville, Kansas.[3] Superman grows up to fight not for truth, justice, and the American way but as Josef Stalin's fighter for global socialism. He still has the red cape and the blue tights, but he bears a hammer and sickle on his chest. With his X-ray vision and super-hearing, he's able to scout out American spies and soldiers as he fights for a Communist utopia. The alien servant-hero story is twisted in ways Americans would find surprising and disturbing.

After reading about the graphic novel in a newsmagazine, I

---

[2]Stephanie Koontz, *The Way We Never Were: American Families and the Nostalgia Trap* (New York: Basic Books, 1992).
[3]Mark Millar, *Superman: Red Son* (New York: DC Comics, 2004).

picked up a copy in a local bookstore and flipped through it, amused. It was a reminder of something we all know but seldom think about. We come to be who we are—all of us—through a complex series of factors. Sorting out who we are and why we're here can be difficult for any of us, but it's a special obstacle for children who don't know much or anything about their biological roots. How much of me is tied up in my genes? How much of it is the result of my upbringing? How much is just my own free decisions? Do I really belong here? Do I belong anywhere?

A sense of acceptance and belonging is the first and most important aspect of growing up after adoption. The most critical part of this—whether you're a parent, child, or other—is how you view the term "adopted." People will often ask me what the key to raising adopted children is. I tell them that honestly, we don't know—we don't have any adopted children. The term "adopted kid" assumes an ongoing difference, something that differentiates him from a "regular kid." That's not what adoption is—at least not adoption that reflects the mystery of Christ.

Our son Jonah was born three and a half weeks premature, but we don't think of him as our "premature baby." We don't introduce our children Benjamin, Timothy, and Samuel and then say, "Here's our premature son Jonah." Jonah is just Jonah. He was premature, yes, and that's part of his story. But it doesn't define who he is. The same is true of those who came into our family by adoption. Adopted is a past-tense verb, not an adjective.

For parents, there are several key facets of maintaining an atmosphere of belonging in their home. The first is simply not to allow adoption to be the key defining characteristic of your child. Don't introduce your child as "my adopted daughter." She's your daughter. One of the saddest testimonies I've ever heard about adoption is from a woman who said that her parents always referred to her as "our daughter" until she disappointed them with some poor choices. They then referred to her as "our adopted daughter." What she could read behind that was the message, "Don't blame us; we're ashamed of her." What must the hearing of such words have done to this woman's understanding of who she is?

Now, of course, there are going to be times when you're speaking of your daughter's adoption—it's nothing to be ashamed of. There are also going to be people—her pediatrician, for instance—who need to know right away about the adoption (so they don't walk down blind alleys of medical family histories, etc.).

When you're asked about the adoption, don't be defensive, as though it's a family secret being uncovered. But you don't need to explain to every stranger the circumstances of how your children came into your family. Think of what would happen to your child's sense of self if every time someone asked, "Is that your little boy?" you responded, "Oh yes, this is our Cesarean section son. He wasn't born naturally but instead came to us via Cesarean section." For most children, that would make them feel different at best, freakish at worst.

I recognize this is easier written than carried out. When our boys were smaller, people in department stores or gas stations would often ask, "Are they twins?" Our response would be, "No, they're three weeks apart." You could almost see the neurons firing in their brains as they stopped to mull that one over. Usually by the time these strangers formulated the "yeah, but, how . . ." rejoinder, we'd already said our good-byes and were on our way. It isn't that we were embarrassed by the question, but we knew our boys were listening, and we didn't want the most important aspect of their personal narrative to be, "We're biologically different." The most important aspect is, "We're family, and we're loved."

The same thing is true when people remark, and they often will, about how a child who was adopted "looks just like" one of his parents or siblings. There's no need to rattle off all the reasons why that can't be true. Simply say, "Thank you. We think she's beautiful."

When adoption happens, all kinds of people will have questions, and they're not afraid to ask them. If you're the parent of a child through adoption, you'll get questions like "Have you ever seen their real dad?" or "How much did they cost?" or "Which ones are adopted?" You don't have to answer all these questions. Simply deflect them with a smile. Some humor helps. Often when meeting new people, they'll ask the "Which ones are adopted?" question. It's just curiosity and doesn't offend me at all. I don't rebuke them—I just answer another question. "Well, this is Benjamin, and he's seven. This is Timothy, and he's seven too. This is Samuel, and he's three. Jonah here is the baby." If a person persists, I'll sometimes laugh and wave it off. "Oh, who can keep track? It doesn't matter to us."

This isn't unique, I've discovered, to families brought together through adoption. When my wife was pregnant with our third child, I learned what many of you have known for years: people will ask a pregnant woman or her husband almost anything. I have had someone ask me, "Do you know where you were when you conceived?" I'll admit I didn't have a response to that one, just a blank and incredulous stare. I've been asked, "How far dilated is your wife?" and other questions of, to me anyway, an uncomfortably gynecological nature. You wouldn't feel obligated to give a detailed obstetric update to total strangers if you were pregnant; you don't need to answer every question curious onlookers ask about adoption either.

Within your home, look for ways to affirm to your child how he belongs. It comes in and out of fashion for parents who've adopted to tell their children they are "chosen children," to emphasize how "special" the children of adoption are. Some parents try to offset any potential feeling of being different by telling the children, "When babies are born, parents just have whomever they get; but we got to pick you out!"

You're not going to warp your child's psyche if you do this, but I don't recommend it. First of all, your job as a parent is already made more difficult by the tendency toward narcissism all around and within us. We all tend to believe already that we're special. As we grow up, televised images of soft-speaking men in sweaters and dancing dinosaurs sing to us that there's never been anyone just like us; they love us "just the way we are."[4] The words then ring a little hollow. Even a four-year-old recognizes eventually that the singing character on television telling him he's special is saying the same thing to everyone.

The "chosen child" language doesn't assuage the troubled hearts of a child who is realizing he was abandoned. As one person puts it, the language raises the question, "Why, for instance, if I were so special, so perfect, did someone give me up?"[5]

Maybe more importantly, the "chosen child" lingo can disrupt the very sense of belonging you're trying to instill. A child can wonder what it was about him that made him so special, what caused you to choose him, and how he can maintain it. Was it how cute he was? How sweet-natured? What, then, happens when he's awkward and pimply and not very cute in his early teenage years? What happens when he's moody and ill-tempered? Your child may have a sense of "survivor's guilt." What happened to all the other children, the ones you rejected because they weren't as cute and cuddly? Could you reject him one day too?

Susanna, a forty-four-year-old woman who had been adopted when she was nine months old, recounted to a group of psychologists something of what being adopted had meant to her. The story her parents had told her had left her with anxieties all her life. They were walking along the cribs filled with babies at an orphanage, they'd told her, until "little Susanna pulled herself up to a standing position, smiled at them, and reached out to them." This story haunted Susanna. She asks herself, what if she'd been in a foul mood that day? What if her diaper had needed changing, and she was sulking in the corner of her crib? Susanna said she asks herself, "Would they have chosen that smiler down the row?" What a question.

The kind of belonging and acceptance you want your child to be able to recognize, though, in the fullness of time, is not a self-focused,

---

[4]Jeff Zaslow, "Blame It on Mr. Rogers: Why Young Adults Feel So Entitled," *Wall Street Journal*, July 5, 2007, B5.
[5]Sandra J. Higgs, "The Pain of Being Adopted: One Adoptee's Journey," *Journal of Pastoral Care* 47 (1993): 375.

merit-based sense of belonging but a gracious one instead. That's, after all, the way our Father adopted us. It was emphatically not, as God tells the Israelites, "because you were more in number than any other people that the LORD set his love on you and chose you, for you were the fewest of all peoples" (Deut. 7:7). The Bible reminds us that not many of us "were wise according to worldly standards, not many were powerful, not many were of noble birth" (1 Cor. 1:26). So why did God choose to save us, to pursue us with the gospel in the first place? It's all due, simply, to what the Scriptures call his "good pleasure" (Eph. 1:5, KJV). You want your child, however he or she came into your family, to grow up knowing what it means to be loved apart from "earning" that love through "performance"—even just the "performance" of being "special."

A couple told me once of adopting a young girl from an Asian country where she'd had a regimen of working for her food. She'd been expected to scrub floors, make her bed, and clean toilets for the right to the benefits of a place to sleep and a spot at the table. This couple relayed how difficult it was to break her of this pattern. She would almost compulsively clean and kept telling her new parents what a "hard worker" she was, as though to justify her presence in the household. Of course, her parents would expect her, as a member of the family, to contribute to the work of the house—to help her parents clean up, to keep her room tidy, and so forth. But first they had to teach her that such things were because she was a welcomed member of the family, not a maid earning her room and board. For her parents, the little girl's cleaning her room—doing all the things that make me happy when I see my sons doing them now—made them sad. The clean room was beside the point; it was the motive behind it that troubled them, a heart that couldn't believe she could be loved.

Even if you chose your child from a "lineup" of children, emphasize the good providence of God in putting your family together. You might say, "God chose to bring you into our family through adoption. He chose to bring Maggie into her family through birth. Isn't

it great how our God brings families together? We are so happy he
knew that you were to be our child!"

Children who've been adopted are going to, of course, show some
differences from the rest of the family in some areas. These could be
obvious or subtle. Acknowledge your child's unique gifts without
making him feel isolated from the rest of the family. If everyone in
your family is less than five feet tall, and your son is six-foot-seven,
play basketball with him—even though you'll lose—and rejoice that
your family finally has a basketball player. Don't just point out the
ways he's different, though. Point out the ways he is part of what
makes your family your family.

Remember that God designed families so children could grow up
to be like their parents. This isn't mere biology. Disciples grow up
to be like their teachers (Luke 6:40), and there's no blood tie there.
Little boys want to mimic their fathers and see themselves as being
like their fathers. Little girls do the same with their mothers. Be
attentive to the ways that's the case in your situation, and be creative.
Don't force your child to fit into some preexisting mold, but find the
points of commonality that already naturally exist.

My son Timothy likes to drink coffee because he knows I do.
We'll go to the coffee shop together and drink coffee. His is decaf-
feinated and is mostly milk, but the effect's the same. He'll say all
the time, "We're the ones who drink coffee, aren't we, Dad?" In a
picture frame behind the desk where I'm typing this is a picture that
Timothy drew of him and me drinking our coffee, along with the
scrawled words, "You and me drinking coffee. I like you." Benjamin,
on the other hand, knows I like politics. He sits up with me on election nights, watching the returns on television, and handicaps what
candidate is going to win what places.

These little convergences are going to differ from family to family and from child to child. Watch for them. If you're a Baltimore
Orioles fan, see if your child is interested too. If so, talk about how
you and he are just alike—you both like the Orioles. If your daughter

likes to bicycle alongside you, talk about all the people in your family who like to bicycle, just like her.

In my family, my grandmother was continually speaking about who got what traits from whom. If one of us threw down a toy in anger, she'd nod her head, knowingly. "Oh yes," she'd say, "he got that temper from Uncle Buford. Buford was mild as water, but when he'd had enough, he'd had enough." When one of us was excited about Christmas, she'd say, "You got that from your grandfather. He loved Christmas." Well, it didn't take me long to figure out that any child will throw a toy down, given enough provocation, and just about everybody loves Christmas. You don't really need a genetic explanation for those things. But what was she doing? She was communicating, "You're one of us." Find ways to communicate this message to all your children, including those who were adopted.

Also show that you love and respect the differences between you and your child, whether those differences are the result of adoption or just the way things are. This can be especially important when the child's distinctiveness in the family is immediately obvious—say, in the case of cross-racial adoption. One expert on transracial adoption notes, for instance, that one issue that repeatedly comes up in her interviews with women who have been adopted is the issue of hair. Now, at first glance nothing seems more trivial—especially to a man like me, with no daughters—than the issue of styling hair. To the women this expert consulted, though, it meant a great deal. The African-American women often had hair that was to be treated differently than "white hair."[6]

In such cases, the most loving thing a mother can do is to learn from African-American friends how to treat her daughter's hair, or vice versa in the case of African-American parents with a Caucasian or Asian or Latino daughter. As the mother (or father, I suppose, but probably more often the mother) cares for her daughter's hair, she can tell her how beautiful her hair is, and how marvelous it is that

[6]Sandra Patton, *BirthMarks: Transracial Adoption in Contemporary America* (New York: New York University Press, 2000), 80.

God created us with so many wonderful differences, how delighted
he is in them. Such things as a mother braiding her daughter's hair
or a father teaching his son how to deal with racial discrimination
signal to children the kind of protection and provision God designed
for parents to give. It also teaches children to be attentive to the dis-
tinctive needs of others so that when they grow up in Christ, they too
may in humility count others as more significant than themselves by
looking out for others' interests (Phil. 2:3–4).

One key aspect of communicating belonging and acceptance
has to do with teaching about adoption itself. Your children are
going to hear some horrible messages about adoption in the popular culture, including in some places you'd never expect, from Walt
Disney to Dr. Seuss. Take those opportunities to teach about how
your understanding of adoption is rooted in the gospel itself. If your
child reads or watches, for instance, *The Jungle Book*, he might
grow fearful about the circumstances of Mowgli's "adoption." He is
a "man-child" raised by wolves but has to go back to the world of
humans because he doesn't belong with the wolves. Don't be afraid
of this conversation. Read the story or watch the movie and then
say, "Mowgli wasn't really adopted, was he? He grew up with the
wolves, but he wasn't a wolf. He didn't belong. That's not like you.
You're a child of Adam, made in the image of God, and so are your
mommy and daddy. You'll always belong with us."

This is the kind of reinterpreting you'll be doing all the time
anyway, if you're a discerning parent. Children who read the nursery
rhyme "Peter, Peter, Pumpkin Eater" don't usually grow up to hold
their wives hostage, and readers of *Where the Wild Things Are* civi-
lize just as easily as those who don't. Parents signal which aspects of
media represent reality and which don't.

Highlight for your child how grateful you are to God for what
he's done in the adoption. One useful time for us has been a special
holiday. The date the boys legally became ours is as big a celebration
(maybe bigger) as a birthday. We've established rituals, rooted in the
adoption itself. We always eat roasted chicken, since that's what we

ate every day in Russia. We give gifts (and not just to the "adopted" ones). We take a short day-trip to do something fun, perhaps to the children's museum in nearby Indianapolis or the zoo in Cincinnati or to a cabin on a lake nearby. Around the dinner table, we recount the story, and we thank God for adopting all of us and allowing us to be together as a family. We call it "Moore Day" since this was the day the boys became Moores, and our entire extended family recognizes it just like a birthday. Your celebrations will probably look different from ours, but find some way to create family traditions that mark the adoption as a blessing.

Above all, as parents, find ways to mimic the fatherhood of God in this. As we've seen earlier, our God through his Spirit "bears witness with our spirit that we are children of God" (Rom. 8:16). He repeatedly announced to Jesus some version of "You are my beloved Son." Do the same. Take the time to snuggle up with your little girl and say, "I am so glad you're my daughter." Crawl into the bed with your son and whisper, "I'm so glad I'm your mommy." Tell them often, in happy times and in stressful times alike, "I'll always love you, and you'll always be welcome here, no matter what you do." From the very start, hold your child. Show physical affection and love.

Friends and fellow church members can help families with this sense of belonging and acceptance. They shouldn't ask questions, especially in front of the children, about the adoption, unless it's readily apparent why. One awkward and frightening time that repeatedly comes up for children who've been adopted is in classrooms, whether in elementary school or church Bible study classes, when teachers ask students to bring baby pictures or draw family trees. Recognize that you may have children who've been adopted in your room—maybe that you don't even know about—and that some of them don't have baby pictures. When it comes to the family tree, the solution is much easier. Their family tree is the tree onto which they've been grafted. You might say, "Draw the family tree of the family into which you've been born or adopted so you can see your heritage." If you're a Bible study, Sunday school, or Christian academy teacher, follow up this project with having the entire class draw the family tree into which all Christ-followers have been adopted—the genealogy of Jesus from the New Testament (don't try this if you are a public schoolteacher).

Raising children after adoption is one thing. Growing up after adoption is another. Perhaps you're reading this as an older adolescent or as an adult who was adopted. Maybe you're friends with or are married to someone in that situation. The question of belonging can be one of the most troublesome issues you face in life.

First, recognize that in some ways your situation is no different than everyone else's. That's not easy to see, of course, since you only know your experience. You may assume that "regular people" all feel perfect kinship with their families and sense a cozy feeling of belonging all the time. It's not so.

One of the most manipulative and disingenuous evangelistic appeals I've ever heard came from a traveling evangelist who spoke at a "youth night" service in a church where I served as associate pastor. He said to the throngs of teenagers he'd attracted with free pizza, "Some of you just feel out of sorts right now. You feel like your parents don't understand you, like nobody understands you, like you don't fit in anywhere. You just feel like you don't even know who you are anymore. If so, pray this prayer after me." This appeal was nauseating because *every* teenager feels this way. It's not an indication of one's spiritual condition. But teenagers all over the room were thinking, "It sounds like he's talking directly to me!"

Every human being feels at some point, and many people for most of their lives, as though he or she can't find the niche in which he or she belongs. It's not just you. Every person looks at his relatives and thinks, "I am nothing like these people," regardless of biological relatedness. This is why Christmas and Thanksgiving dinners are so stressful in many homes. It might be that some of your loneliness and identity crisis is less about being adopted and more about being human.

There are, though, some special challenges for you if you've been adopted when it comes to receiving your belonging and acceptance in your family. The "who am I?" and "what if?" questions can, if you let them, lead you to want to isolate yourself from your family. If you know Christ, though, meditate on the providence of God in your personal story. You belong because you are exactly where God intended you to be, in order to become the person you are. Nothing happens to you by accident. All things are part of a secret drama in which everything works together "according to the counsel of his will" (Eph. 1:11).

If you've been adopted, there's been no accident. You have the genes God wanted you to have. You have the parents God wanted you to have. The interplay between the two makes you who you are. Despite all the reductionisms of our age, we come to be the kind of persons we are by a curious combination of genes, upbringing, and free decisions. In your case, as in the case of all of us, God orchestrated all these factors to form you into the kind of person you are, with the kinds of experiences you have.

Why? You may not know for thousands of years. If you're in Christ, God is preparing you to rule over the cosmos. He wants you to be who you are in Christ and to be ready for this reign. Receive God's formation of who you are in this way with thanksgiving.

Our personalities, like our bodies, are formed mysteriously. Just as God formed you "fearfully and wonderfully" in your birth mother's womb, he also directed you into your new household. "My frame was not hidden from you, when I was being made in secret, intricately woven in the depths of the earth," David sings. "Your eyes saw my unformed substance; in your book were written, every one of them, the days that were formed for me, when as yet there was none of them" (Ps. 139:15–16). The same is true of your story, your background.

Whether you had loving parents or disastrous ones, you're accepted in your household in Christ. Whether your parents understand you or not, your Father knows you. He knows every inclination of your heart, better than you do. You belong.

BEHAVIOR AND DISCIPLINE

A couple of years ago, I read in our local newspaper about a woman with a terminal disease. She knew she just had months to live. She also had small children at home. When asked what were the most difficult parts of living a life she knew would soon be over, I was stunned by her answer. She said it was hard for her to discipline her children. She was aware that every moment was forming their last memories of her, memories that would have to last them a lifetime. She didn't want those memories to be of a time-out over who hit whom with whose toy. She knew, though, that she had to discipline them. She was their mother, and if she didn't, who would?

The ambivalence about discipline in this woman's situation was poignant because, if we think about it honestly, it's true to a certain extent of all of us. We're all terminally ill in that we know that "it is appointed for man to die once, and after that comes judgment" (Heb. 9:27). Can't every parent relate to this dying woman's dread at hearing her own voice having to rebuke and correct?

Discipline can be a difficult issue in growing up after adoption, first of all, because often a family is formed so suddenly. If you adopt a newborn baby, your situation will be virtually identical to those who biologically give birth. You'll have months of a child who does little more than sleep, eat, cry, and gaze into your eyes. You have time to get to know your child and to think through your philosophy of discipline, to allow yourself to be shaped by the Word and the Spirit into one who disciplines with grace and mercy. You ease into the task of direction and correction of behavior. For those of you who adopt older children though—and by older I mean toddlers and above—discipline is going to be an awkward transition for you in many ways.

When you adopt, you don't usually have time to feel like a parent before you have to start acting like one, teaching and training children as to your expectations for their behavior. Sometimes adopting parents assume, wrongly, that they should wait to discipline until someday way off in the future.

When we first arrived home with Benjamin and Timothy, we followed counsel given to us to immediately put into place certain boundaries for them. If they tried to go toward the stairs or pick up the coasters to bang on the coffee table, we'd say in a gentle but firm voice, "No, no" and redirect them to another place in the room. My father thought such rules were ridiculous. "Haven't they been through enough?" he said. "They've been in a Russian orphanage for a year, bless their hearts. If they want to bang up that coffee table, well, just let them have at it. You can buy a new coffee table."

My father was simply moving into his grandparent stage—"Just love them through it." This was a strikingly new attitude for him, but I'd been warned it was on its way. If we'd followed his counsel on this matter, though, I probably would be writing a different book today—*How a Christian Dad Loves His Convicted Arsonist Children* or something like that. These cherubic little ex-orphans would always have the sympathy of his heart, regardless of how old or how undisciplined they became. We had a different responsibility though—to raise these boys up into men.

Of course, our mode of discipline was by necessity age-appropriate. You don't expect from a toddler what you'd expect from an older child, and you don't discipline in the same way either. But it would have been cruel if we hadn't let the boys know, by teaching them from the very beginning, what we expected of them. How could we allow them to pull the stuffing out of the couch for two months and then suddenly rebuke them for doing so?

There's a temptation for many adopting parents to "make it all up" to the child for the years and the love he's lost. These parents then turn the entire focus of their lives and of their home on the child. I remember one couple whose house Maria and I visited, only to see when we walked through the door a life-size oil painting of the little girl they'd adopted, with external light shining on her visage. I don't know if it was the bounce of the light or if it was painted on, but

I'm pretty sure I saw a halo around her pigtails. The temptation for some adopting parents is to prove their love for their new child by laxity in discipline and by indulging in whatever the child wants, be it food or toys or behavior.

This is terribly counterproductive, though. Discipline is one of the ways, as God designed it, that children know they are legitimate and loved parts of the family (Heb. 12:8–10). Moreover, without teaching, instruction, and discipline a child doesn't grow up to recognize the gospel—a gospel that is about, after all, subduing one's own appetites and following after Another (Deut. 8:1–10). If you refuse to discipline, you're preaching a false gospel to your child, a gospel that ignores the fact that God evaluates behavior and that actions have consequences.

Moreover, there's a great distinction between demonstrating love to a child and turning him into the singular focus of the family. The kind of (often guilt-produced) showering of affluence on children actually, counterintuitively, leads to alienation. Children need to know they're loved. They need also to see themselves as useful parts of the family, learning to contribute in small, age-appropriate ways to the household economy. And they need to see themselves as part of a larger story, the security of a family.

Another common problem in the behavior and discipline area has to do with parents, families, and communities who are, for lack of a better word, scared of children who've been adopted. The myth of the maladjusted "adopted" kid is everywhere present, especially among people who don't know many persons who've been adopted.

You'll hear often from adopting parents who immediately blame all behavioral and discipline problems on the circumstances of the adoption. Sometimes parents will panic about "attachment disorder" because the child is mischievous or strong-willed.

Now, bonding and attachment are indeed important aspects of the parent-child relationship, and if you think there's something wrong there, consult your family doctor and your adoption agency for resources. In the vast majority of cases, however, parents are simply identifying the normal range of differences in children, or they're blaming bad behavior or uninformed parenting on a "syndrome." This isn't unique to adoption. Haven't you known parents who always offer, "He's cutting a tooth" or "She's really tired" or "I think he has oppositional-defiance disorder" when one of their children misbehaves in public? There may indeed be factors involved in misbehavior, but in the vast majority of instances, a child's misbehavior is explained by Genesis, not genes; by Eden, not adoption.

Some parents will think a more aloof child hasn't bonded simply because he's not as cuddly as other children they've seen. In many instances, this is simply the result of his personality. Don't we all know (and aren't some of us) the kind of person who doesn't hug easily? This doesn't mean he's cunningly waiting until he's old enough to murder you in your bed. It may mean he's just a shier kind of person. That's who he is, and that's fine.

Just as it is common to under-discipline children who've been adopted, it's just as common for parents to try to over-discipline them. I am not here referring to abuse. Any kind of abuse is always an abomination to God. If you know of anyone abusing a child, whether the child was adopted or not, immediately alert the authorities and, if the person claims to be a Christian, the church authorities as well. Here I am speaking of a lack of patience, an expectation that children should be well-behaved and well-adjusted at an accelerated pace.

This was the problem in my case. I was gentle and loving with the children, but I was constantly correcting misbehavior—including those things that weren't defiance or disobedience, just immaturity. My problem was as simple, and as devilish, as pride. I didn't want to be embarrassed. I didn't want all those people who thought our adopting was foolish to be proven right. I wanted them to see two smiling, well-behaved sons who immediately knew how to shake a man's hand and look him in the eye, who right away knew how to sit quietly through church. I was an idiot. My expectations were unrealistic, sinful, and my problem, not my boys'.

The root of impatience in discipline is really the same as that of overindulgence. In both instances, parents want to "make up for lost time," to speed up a process that takes time. The same Scriptures that command parents to discipline their children also command fathers not to "provoke your children to anger, but bring them up in the discipline and instruction of the Lord" (Eph. 6:4). Like adoption, discipline isn't made up as we go along. It reflects something cosmic and ancient. If you are capricious or harsh in your discipline, you are lying about God's fatherhood. If you yell at your children, you're not reflecting a God who lovingly, joyously, and rationally disciplines his children. If you discipline in anger, you're signaling a God who disciplines not for our good but out of his own frustration.

If you adopt a child or children, though, you'll find your patience tested—sometimes, especially early on, even more than you would in "normal" parenting circumstances. What an opportunity to model the gentle, interested patience of God. Our Father doesn't ignore us in any aspect of our lives, but he doesn't ramrod us into maturity either. "As a father shows compassion to his children, so the LORD shows compassion to those who fear him," David sings. "For he knows our frame; he remembers that we are dust" (Ps. 103:13–14).

Parents who adopt may find themselves with a toddler who, like one of ours, throws the most horrific fits in the middle of the grocery store. Love him, teach him, disciple him toward self-control. But don't allow your discipline to be directed by your sense of personal embarrassment. This isn't about you. Parents may find themselves with an older child who sneaks cigarettes behind the church youth center or uses profanity in his dinner table prayer to bless the food. Deal with the issues, but do so with patience, understanding, and with the end—Christlike maturity—always in view.

While avoiding attributing any behavioral issues to adoption, you do want to craft your disciplinary strategy around the ways your child has been affected or wounded by the circumstances that brought him to you. No child wants, at first, to go to a nursery at your church or to a friend's house for babysitting, and you'll want to avoid these things until you can discern that your child is upset about your leaving, not fearful that you're leaving him for good. Whatever the behavioral issues involved, make sure that your child—regardless of how old or how young—knows you will never leave him or forsake him. Adoption is similar to marriage in this respect. If divorce is an option in your mind—even just a last resort—you are probably going to get divorced. If abandonment is an option, you will never endure what it takes to bring a child to maturity. Your child's been left once, for whatever reason. Make sure he knows you're here to stay.

If you're not an adopting parent or a candidate for becoming one, you might be tempted to assume that all this talk about discipline is irrelevant to you. You'd be wrong. Child-rearing is your business too. That's why the Holy Spirit includes directives about discipline and parenting in Scriptures given to the whole people of God. As you minister to families who've adopted, think deeply about the Word of God on this, and so help spur others on to godliness. If you're an older man or woman with experience in this area, take aside a younger couple and give counsel in a loving, gentle way if you see that it's needed.

DEALING WITH THE PAST

On our living room wall, a picture hangs—some arranged dried flowers behind glass. If you sat in the room, you probably wouldn't notice it at all. It looks just like a typical knick-knack, maybe given as a wedding present or a housewarming gift. I love it. And I hate it. My mother-in-law, who'd traveled with us to Russia, gathered these wildflowers growing between the cracks in the pavement outside the orphanage. When she saw that little burst of color seeping up from the cold, gray, cracking sidewalk, she couldn't help but pick them.

When we arrived home, she pressed the flowers and arranged them into this gift for us. Sometimes I find myself standing in front of it, staring at the flowers. I can see my own reflection in the glass, and I notice that sometimes the reflection is smiling, and sometimes it's pushing away tears. The flowers remind me of that orphanage, of how wounded, how abandoned my boys were. But they also remind me of God's kindness in delivering them to us as our children.

As we've discussed earlier, adoption is always tragic. There's always a dark story underlying it—be it abandonment or death or sickness or poverty or anything else. Those things can be hard to talk about, especially to a little face looking up at you asking, "Why?" It's normal and natural for children to wonder, "Where did I come from?" and "How did I get here?"

Some adopting parents don't have to answer many questions. The child was older when adopted, and he knows—all too well—the circumstances behind the adoption. These children may not have to ask "what," but they're probably wondering "why." Others adopt children so young they don't remember anything about life apart from their parents. It hasn't occurred to them yet to wonder what happened to get them here. But they will. Again, the issue here can't simply be psychological adjustment, although that's important. Parents and children in Christian homes will want to explore the past in ways consistent with the redemptive power of the gospel.

This means, first, that parents must be honest. As we discussed earlier, previous generations erred in assuming adoption was something shameful to be hidden in the dark secrets of the family's history. Don't wait to tell your child he was adopted. If he was an infant, speak of adoption—in positive terms—from as early as he's able to communicate. This is often done best through bedtime or dinner table stories—how God gave you to Mommy and Daddy.

This can be especially complicated if the family has children who came into the home through typical "biological" means. A child may see ultrasound photos of his little sister or be watching as his mother's midsection expands with his growing new sibling. He's naturally going to ask, "Was I in your tummy too?" There's no need for defensiveness or shame here. Answer in an upbeat tone of voice along the lines of, "No, God decided to put you in Chicago (or Guatemala or wherever), and then he sent us to go and find you." Children of a very young age will think little of this. Much of the birth process is a mystery to them anyway, and coming from an orphanage makes as much sense to them as coming from inside a mother.

Some of the questions children ask are more alarming to the parents than to the children precisely because the children aren't operating with the same kind of knowledge of human reproduction. A child might wonder why his parents seem to sweat and clear their throats when he's asking a simple question of geography. In this sense, it can be like a four-year-old who asks his mother what the "virgin birth" is. Dismissing the question can lead to an unorthodox Christology, but too much information can overwhelm a child who thinks, well, that every birth is a virgin birth.

Make sure, then, that whatever you are teaching your child is commensurate with his maturity level. You must be honest, but you need not reveal all the details at once. You will want, again, to image the fatherhood of God in this. God tells us honestly about our past. But God doesn't deposit his revelation all at once, just east of Eden. Instead God speaks for thousands of years "at many times in many ways" until in "these last days" he speaks to us in Christ (Heb. 1:1–2). God speaks to his people through the Law, as to one "under guardians and managers until the date set by his father" (Gal. 4:2). He does this patiently, until "the fullness of time" (Gal. 4:4). It isn't until the last days that God reveals his "plan for the fullness of time" (Eph. 1:10). This mystery of Christ "was not made known to the sons of men in other generations as it has now been revealed to his holy apostles and prophets by the Spirit" (Eph. 3:5).

Now, God did reveal Christ. Every word of Scripture is about Christ and God's plan for the world in Christ. God speaks truthfully and honestly at every stage of revelation. But in Christ all the promises and all the warnings, all the blessings and all the curses, all the types and shadows all come together and find their coherence in him.

In the same way, reveal the truth to your child honestly, at each step he is able to handle. This will differ from child to child. Know your child, where his maturity level is. Don't refuse to answer any question, but fill in the details to greater degree as the child progresses in knowledge, understanding, and maturity.

There is almost never a reason to tell a pre-teen child, for example, that he was conceived due to a rape or that his birth father is imprisoned for murdering his mother. He does deserve that information—it's part of his story—but he doesn't need it now.

Honesty means you have to be willing to say, "I don't know" to some questions, perhaps to many of them. This may be about questions you simply don't know the facts about: "What did my birth mother look like?" or "What was my birth father's name?" or "Did I have any brothers or sisters?" Even more importantly, though, it means you'll have to say, "I don't know" to some "why" questions. The most heart-tearing question of all is, "Why did my mother give me up?" For many parents, the answer has to be, "I don't know."

For most people, theodicy questions—the issue of how God can be just in a world filled with evil—don't emerge until sometime after adulthood. One may question the goodness of God when her boyfriend is killed in a car accident or when he watches a film about the Holocaust. After adoption, though, the theodicy question often emerges much, much earlier. For Christ-following parents, this can be an opportunity to model the way a child of God looks at such things. Don't minimize evil and suffering—acknowledge that these things are really sad and awful. But show your children what it looks like to rest in the fact that whatever others, including even the satanic powers, may mean for evil, God is turning around for the good (Gen. 50:20). In the face of some evil, including some questions about the past involving adoption, all we can do is, like Job before us, trust God and put our hands over our mouths in worshipful awe (Job 42:1–6).

Explaining birth parents and abandonment is often particularly sensitive because it's not simply the child who is threatened by this information. Some parents through adoption are threatened by the thought of these elusive people returning onto the scene. Sometimes you may know so much about them that it's difficult to have much sympathy for the choices they've made. It is very important, though, that you avoid either deifying or demonizing the birth parents.

Some parents try to "rescue" the reputation of a child's birth parents in ways that aren't ultimately helpful. Imagine the confusion it can cause a child, for instance, to hear you explain why her birth parent gave her away, "She couldn't afford a baby." Your daughter may wrack herself with worry about your finances. What happens if you can't afford to take care of her any longer?

At the same time, don't pass judgment on the birth mother or birth father. These people were father and mother to your child in the beginning. Honor them as such. They could have snuffed out her life, especially in this age of easy abortion. Don't succumb to the temptation to cast these former parents in a negative light, even as you sympathize with your child in his anger at them. As Betsy Keefer and Jayne Schooler point out, it's counterproductive to make comments such as, "If your mother had any sense in choosing boyfriends, you never would have been abused." A better response is their suggested alternative, "I'm glad that we are able to keep you safe now."[7]

Instead, seek to model your God, who is both "just and the justifier of the one who has faith in Jesus" (Rom. 3:26). God doesn't ignore the reality of our sin, but he covers it himself, through the blood of the cross.

If you are or someday become a parent to a child through adoption, recognize that a child's fantasies about his birth parents are common and natural. A child is able to project all his hopes and wishes onto a perfectly understanding, perfectly loving parent, someone who "really understands" and can rescue her from her situation.[8] The child might imagine that his birth parents were royalty or sports heroes or

---

[7]Betsy Keefer and Jayne E. Schooler, *Telling the Truth to Your Adopted or Foster Child: Making Sense of the Past* (Westport, CT: Bergin & Garvey, 2000), 90.
[8]Ronald J. Nydam, "Fantasy and Hope in the Lives of Adoptees," *Journal of Pastoral Care* 51 (1997): 65–78.

just the kind of people who will allow one to talk on the phone past 11 at night. This doesn't mean you are being rejected as a parent. In fact, isn't it common for most children, in any situation, to fantasize about having perfect parents (perhaps, as in my case as a child, the mom and dad on *The Brady Bunch*)? Listen to the fantasies of your child. What he's telling you about his "real family" can sometimes tell you simply what he's wishing for in his own life, what he thinks is missing.

The pain of abandonment is real, and it will become pronounced. This, again, is not rejection of the parents via adoption. As scholar Ronald Nydam demonstrates, for one who has been adopted, "relinquishment" or abandonment is a very different category than that of adoption.[9] A child can hate the fact he was abandoned, can grieve the loss of his birth mother, and still be glad you're his parents.

If you were adopted, chances are you'll want to try to find out about your birth family. You may even wish to initiate contact with them. This is not an act of disrespect to your parents in any way. Be patient with them, though. Your parents may see this as rejection, even if they don't say it. They may fear that you'll leave them to be someone else's son or daughter. If you do decide to search out your birth parents, be sure to honor your father and mother—the ones who raised you—in the process. Turn the tables on your parents and patiently reassure them that they're your *real* parents and always will be.

Know, though, that finding your birth parents will still leave a lot to mystery. You may discover where that birthmark came from or from where you inherited that throat-clearing habit. You might see what you'll look like in a few years, with a few more pounds and a receding hairline. Finding your birth parents, though, won't tell you who you are. Who you are has been forged by more than genes, coming also from thousands of dinner table conversations, hallway arguments, church group retreats, quiet moments of prayer, and much more. Above all, you are who you are in Christ.

---

[9]Ronald J. Nydam, *Adoptees Come of Age: Living within Two Families* (Louisville: Westminster/John Knox, 1999), 1–6.

If you were adopted, you will, at some point, feel a sense of help-less rage in the face of abandonment. You may alternate between idealizing your birth parents and hating them. It may take you a lifetime to resolve the struggle in your own soul over this, but one thing is certain if you know and follow a Messiah named Jesus: you must forgive your birth parents.

For too many of us, forgiveness is seen as an act that really spiritual Christians do. That's not the way forgiveness is presented in Scripture though. "Forgive, and you will be forgiven," Jesus tells us (Luke 6:37). Forgiveness doesn't mean you feel that what's been done to you is okay. It doesn't mean you have warm feelings toward the persons forgiven. It means you relinquish the right to exercise vengeance. You rest in the fact that God's justice is carried out by God, either at Judgment Day or at the cross. If your birth parents are in the Christ who took their place, they've already been to hell for abandoning you or abusing you or neglecting you. If they never come to Christ, they'll answer to a God who searches every heart, and he will do what's just. You aren't a vigilante, even within your own mind. You believe in God.

Dealing with the past is probably the saddest aspect of this book for me. Benjamin and Timothy know their story, but so far they haven't asked much about their birth mother. They each know that they grew in another lady's body and that we're grateful to God for these women's protecting them through that time. They don't think of the word *mother* yet as associated with that, so we haven't had to face the question of "Why did she give me up?" But we will. And, I anticipate, it's going to be horrible. How could it be otherwise?

The questions of the past remind us that adoption is always part of a sad story. The flowers framed on my wall remind me of ugli-ness, abandonment, death. They also, though, remind me of beauty, family, life. To an infinitely greater degree, every Christian knows something of this already. We're the people who sing of being lost and now found. We're people who proclaim Christ crucified. We glory, after all, in a Roman torture device that saved the world. All of our pasts include mystery and agony. It's not that we don't weep. It's that we weep knowing those tears will be wiped away by hands scabbed over with nail-prints.

CONCLUSION

Television reruns from yesteryear may give us an unrealistically utopian view of what it's like to grow up after adoption. But popular sentiment all around us all too often gives us an unrealistically apocalyptic view. People speak of rearing "adopted children" with hushed tones and raised eyebrows, as though this task is not for the faint of heart. They speak of the trials of "adopted" children with all their identity crises and hidden hurts, as though one is predestined for misery because of adoption itself.

Those people will always be with us. They're the same ones who tell newly married couples how tough marriage is "once the honeymoon's over, you just wait and see." They're the ones who tell a newly pregnant woman to "get your sleep now, 'cause you won't get any more for eighteen years."

The reality, though, is that in most ways parenting is parenting, and growing up is growing up. It's always hard. Some unique challenges go along with adoption—challenges related to finding a sense of belonging, to discipline and discipleship, to answering questions about origins. Count these as all joy. They point all of us—not just kids who were adopted—to the gospel. The gospel welcomes us and receives us as loved children. The gospel disciplines us and prepares us for eternity as heirs. The gospel speaks truth to us and shows us our misery in Adam and our glory in Christ. The gospel shows us that we were born into death and then shows us, by free grace, that we're adopted for life.

9

Concluding Thoughts

I'M WAITING FOR the sound of footsteps. It's quite early here; the house is still and dark. There are balloons and streamers all over the kitchen, where I am typing this. I know that any minute the morning will ignite as two little feet come running down the stairs. It's Benjamin's birthday. Last night I could hear Benjamin and Timothy whispering in their beds till way past 10. Benjamin was speculating about what he'd get as a present from us, from his grandparents, from his uncles. Timothy tried to hide his envy. His birthday's not for three weeks yet, and for that short time he'll just be six, not seven like his triumphant, (barely) older brother. All I can think about right now, while I wait for Benjamin to wake up, is that seven years ago today my firstborn son was born. In a matter of weeks, his brother was born too. I missed both days.

I didn't send out any "It's a Boy" notices. I didn't deliver flowers to my wife. There was no cardboard stork in our front yard. I wasn't a deadbeat dad; I just wasn't a dad at all. I didn't know my sons were born. Their births went as unnoticed to me as any other pair of foreign babies on the other side of the globe.

As I see Benjamin's wrapped presents on the counter next to me, I wonder, what did he look like that day? What did his newborn cries sound like? Would I recognize him if I heard him then? Did anyone hold him, or was he just washed and placed in a filthy crib? Did his birth mother whisper to him, maybe telling him that she was sorry, but she had to leave him there? I don't know. I never will.

I also wonder what I was doing that day. My old calendar from that year shows that I was working on my doctoral dissertation, typing away like I am right now. I probably walked to my favorite coffee shop and ordered the regular. I was probably also feeling sorry for myself. I don't need a calendar to tell me that. I felt that way every day then.

I'd prayed every morning and every night for children. I would have done so that day too, with a desperate whine to my voice. I didn't know that day that my prayers had been answered, in a way beyond all I could ask or even think. I had no way of knowing that the greatest joys of my life so far were here, and yet not here; already and not yet. God wasn't ignoring me. He was training my affections to love these two boys, to be a father theologically, not just biologically.

It makes me wonder this morning what else I've prayed for that is secretly answered already. In the big scheme of things, everything— literally everything—fits into that category. There's an empty tomb in Jerusalem with no one's name on it, and an empty throne in the New Jerusalem with my new name on it. I still have a lot to learn between now and then.

At the beginning of this book, I invited you to converse with me about adoption, and I mentioned that I don't know who you are. I still don't, of course, but I do know a little better who I am— better than I did this time seven years ago. I'm the man who won't be in a pulpit or a library or a faculty meeting tonight. I'm the man who will be taking another photograph for my wife to glue in some scrapbook. I'm the man who will be repeating, "slow down, one at a time" as an adrenaline-drunk child tears open his presents. I'm the man with the plastic birthday hat on my head. And I'll wear it all evening, even after the kids have taken off theirs. It's my theologian's cap; it's taught me far more about my God and his gospel than the tasseled formal scholar's hat on my shelf ever has.

That's about all I can say because I hear those footfalls now. It's not just two feet, it seems, but maybe six or eight. The birthday boy's so excited, he must be rounding up the others. They'll be excited too. They're brothers, you know. It's time for me to end this because there are some little fellows to chase around the house—in a birthday hat.

I missed the first birthdays, and I won't miss another one, not until the day I die.

As the final words blip across the screen, I am praying for you, whoever you are. Maybe you've been reading this book because for whatever reason you're interested in adoption, but you don't know Christ. Won't you take the time to question whether maybe, just maybe, this stuff is true? Would you read through a section of the Bible, perhaps the Gospel of John, while praying that God would show you the glory of it all, if indeed it is true? Maybe you're convinced of Jesus' claims about himself and about you, but you don't know how to start out a life as his follower. Just call out to God, in whatever words you can find. Ask him to forgive you, to receive you; ask him to count Jesus' crucifixion as your judgment, Jesus' resurrection as your life. I promise you he'll hear you. You only have to start out with two easy syllables: Abba.

Maybe, though, you're a follower of Jesus already, perhaps for a long time now. I pray that you will grow in wonder that you were a cosmic orphan, and now you're the beloved son of the Father, an heir of everything you can see and of things so glorious they'd burn your corneas to powder if you looked at them now. I pray also that you will picture that gospel and that you'll join in this mission of representing Christ to the fatherless among us.

Maybe there are abandoned children languishing right now in cribs somewhere who will be blowing out birthday candles with their new families this time next year because of your witness, your money, or your encouragement. Maybe they'll be yours. I don't know. Like I say, I don't know you. But maybe you're waiting for the sound of footsteps too.

Acknowledgments

I AM A DEBTOR not to the flesh but to the Spirit. Through this project, though, I am much aware of how indebted I am to some brothers and sisters in the Spirit who are very much flesh and blood. My debt starts with Justin Taylor at Crossway Books, who has walked a similar path to fatherhood and who pressed me along this path. I am more grateful to him than he knows. This book would not be possible if not for the diligent and wise labor of my editor at Crossway, Ted Griffin.

This book owes its existence to a community of scholars here at The Southern Baptist Theological Seminary. President R. Albert Mohler Jr. has been a friend and counselor through this entire process. I appreciate more than he knows his bearing with my spotty cell phone service while I tucked away to write in the woods of Brown County, Indiana and his allowing me to hijack routinely his radio program for the cause of adoption during my times of guest hosting. My colleague Dan Dumas, also a dad who knows the joy of adoption, helped secure me a secret, quiet office on our campus in which I could write for a few minutes or hours at a time without interruption. I can never repay that debt. I appreciate the encouragement and the counsel of all my colleagues here, especially Chuck Lawless, Jimmy Scroggins, Clark Logan, Randy Stinson, Tom Schreiner, Greg Wills, and Don Whitney.

I am grateful to my special assistant and beloved friend Robert Sagers who walked with me through this entire project. We must look like one another because people often ask if we are brothers. We are now.

My staff members Brenna Whitley, Elizabeth Honett, and Ashley Smith, my friends Cathy Wills and Jeremy Pierre, and my interns

Jedidiah Coppenger, Phillip Bethancourt, Andrew Walker, Devin Maddox, and Daniel Patterson were of great help to me. I'm especially indebted to Daniel, who faithfully read and marked up multiple copies of each chapter. Daniel let me know that non-southerners probably wouldn't unders d what it means to be "bowed up" or what a "honky-tonk" is. He also helpfully let me know such things as though he's sure *incredibility* is a word, it sounds an awful lot like *strategery* to him.

I'm grateful to my congregation, Highview Baptist Church, for their love and support through this project. Preaching every week through the Gospel of Matthew at our Fegenbush Lane campus has fueled even further my awe at the adopting power of God. I am grateful to my fellow pastors at Highview, especially Corey Abney, Jon Akin, Nick Moore, and Troy Temple and most especially Senior Pastor Kevin Ezell. Kevin's passion for and leadership in adoption mission in the local church is exactly, and I mean *exactly*, what I would love to see happen in churches all over the world.

My editorial board colleagues at *Touchstone: A Journal of Mere Christianity* were also of great help, especially in their comments and suggestions on the article from which this book grew.

I am indebted to my beautiful wife, the mother of my four children, who was never more beautiful than she is to me now. She shouldered much of the parenting while I finished a book on parenting. And I am indebted to our four boys. I don't know which of you are "biological" and which of you were "adopted." I am sorry I've been buried in that basement typing so much. And I promise we'll go bowling now.

Finally, I would never have been able to write this book or to know what this book is about if it weren't for some friends who pooled together money for an adoption for an impoverished young doctoral student and his wife six years ago. To David and Judi Prince, Randy and Danna Stinson, Pete and Vicki Schemm, Danny and Charlotte Akin, Jim and Linda Smith, Darrell and Elaine Cook,

Jerry and Rhonda Johnson, Christopher and Dawn Cowan, Gregory and Kimberly Thornbury, Tom and Margaret Nettles, Tim and Michelle Harrelson, and Mark and Tiffanie Overstreet, all I can say is, thank you.

On this list is one anonymous couple who asked never to be named. You are not anonymous to my heart or to my God. May he repay you a thousandfold in this age and in the age to come.

Scripture Index

General Index

RUSSELL D. MOORE is Dean of the School of Theology and Senior Vice President for Academic Administration at The Southern Baptist Theological Seminary. He also serves as a preaching pastor at Highview Baptist Church in Louisville, Kentucky. Dr. Moore and his wife, Maria, have four sons.